Ten G

Books by Zen Master Seung Sahn

Dropping Ashes on the Buddha

Only Don't Know

Ten Gates

Wanting Enlightenment Is a Big Mistake

TEN GATES

*The Kong-an Teaching of
Zen Master Seung Sahn*

REVISED EDITION
EDITED BY
Zen Master Dae Kwang

FOREWORD BY
Robert Aitken

Shambhala
Boston & London
2007

Shambhala Publications, Inc.
Horticultural Hall
300 Massachusetts Avenue
Boston, Massachusetts 02115
www.shambhala.com

9 8 7 6 5 4 3 2 1
Revised Edition
Printed in the United States of America

♾ This edition is printed on acid-free paper that meets the
American National Standards Institute z39.48 Standard.

Distributed in the United States by Random House, Inc.,
and in Canada by Random House of Canada Ltd

Interior design and composition: Greta D. Sibley & Associates

Library of Congress Cataloging-in-Publication Data
Sungsan Tae Sŏnsa.
Ten gates: the kong-an teaching of Zen master Seung Sahn.
p. cm.
ISBN 978-1-59030-417-4 (alk. paper)
1. Koan. 2. Zen meditations. I. Title.
BQ9287.4.s86 2007
294.3'44—DC22
2007010078

Contents

Foreword by Robert Aitken, Roshi   vii

Introduction by Zen Master Dae Kwang   ix

Ten Gates: A Poem by Zen Master Seung Sahn   xvii

FIRST GATE
JoJu's Dog
1

SECOND GATE
JoJu's Washing the Bowls
7

THIRD GATE
Seong Am Calls Master
18

FOURTH GATE
Bodhidharma Has No Beard
28

FIFTH GATE
Hyang Eom's "Up a Tree"
37

SIXTH GATE
Dropping Ashes on the Buddha
46

Contents

SEVENTH GATE
Ko Bong's Three Gates
59

EIGHTH GATE
Duk Sahn Carrying His Bowls
71

NINTH GATE
Nam Cheon Kills a Cat
85

TENTH GATE
Mouse Eats Cat Food
98

ELEVENTH GATE
Man Gong's Net
112

TWELFTH GATE
Seung Sahn's Three Men Walking
114

The Third Interview by Jerry Shepherd
117

APPENDIX 1
Notes on the Zen Masters of the Ten Gates
121

APPENDIX 2
Biography of Zen Master Seung Sahn
123

APPENDIX 3
Glossary
125

How Are You?
A Foreword

Soen Sa Nim begins his letters by asking, "How are you?" and his students take up the question too. "How are you?" they ask in turn in their letters to their teacher. We begin to notice this most routine of American greetings as though for the first time.

Does Soen Sa Nim's "How are you?" differ from his students' "How are you?" Is their "How are you?" just an echo? Are they being imitation Soen Sa Nims? If so, that won't do. Soen Sa Nim stands on his own feet, you stand on yours, I stand on mine.

If you stand on your own feet, then what do you say? "Fine!" might be all right, or maybe you are just temporizing. *Temporizing*—there's an interesting word. It means you are gaining time, but gaining time for what? The next question and the next temporizing? When will you come to terms?

"How are you?" "Fine!" That's more like it. There are other questions like this in this book. Please pay attention.

—*Robert Aitken*
Koko An Zendo, Honolulu
Spring Training Period, 1987

Introduction by
Zen Master Dae Kwang

The kong-an (Ch., *kung-an;* Jp., *koan*) is a unique and distinctive feature of the Zen tradition that sets it immediately apart not only from other Buddhist meditation practices, but also from all other spiritual traditions.

A kong-an is a seemingly illogical question posed by a Zen teacher to awaken a student. During the golden age of Zen creativity in the Tang dynasty in China (618–907), teachers and students lived in close proximity and spontaneously confronted each other in everyday life situations. One famous kong-an involved a student approaching Zen Master Dong Sahn while he was weighing flax and asking, "What is Buddha?" Dong Sahn replied, "Three pounds of flax." The clarity and directness of the reply—its quality of pointing directly to mind—made it valuable as a teaching tool even beyond that immediate situation. It was remembered, recorded, and used over and over again.

For the practitioners of that era, it was like living on the razor's edge—one could not afford to be slothful. In those days every person could be both teacher and student at the same time. Every exchange, no matter how innocuous, was a potential minefield and a test of one's attainment of the enlightened mind. There were numerous instances when the exchange between teacher and student helped the student reach enlightenment.

Such exchanges were avidly recounted all over China and became part of Zen folklore. It was not until the Sung dynasty

(960–1280) that the exchanges were formally recorded and organized into collections, then commented on and used as teaching tools by generations of Zen teachers. The two most important collections of kong-ans are still in use by Zen teachers today. The *Blue Cliff Record* (Ch., *Pi-yen-lu;* Jp., *Hekigan-Roku*) was compiled in 1125 and was similar to the Models of the Elders gathered by the monk Hsueu-tou (988–1052). A century later the *Gateless Gate* (Ch., *Wu-men-kuan;* Jp., *Mumonkan*) appeared, collected by the monk Hui-kai (1184–1260).

Today, the body of traditional kong-ans numbers 1,750. From these, Zen Master Seung Sahn selected ten, which he calls the Ten Gates and through which he requires his students to pass. The Ten Gates represent the various styles of kong-ans to be found among the 1,750. Zen Master Seung Sahn explains:

> Many kong-ans are quite similar. From among all the kong-ans I have chosen ten which are representative of all the different types and show a distinctive style. So the Ten Gates are like a map to all the traditional 1,750 kong-ans.

For example, there are four kinds of "like-this" kong-ans:

1. "Without like this" kong-ans: true emptiness, silence, complete stillness.
2. "Become-one like this" kong-ans: KATZ, hit, etc.
3. "Only like this" kong-ans: the meaning is truth— "When spring comes, the grass grows by itself."
4. "Just like this" kong-ans: just doing is truth—go drink tea, wash your bowls, etc.

There are also "opposites questions" kong-ans that address issues like good and bad. There are kong-ans that teach "moment to moment keep correct situation, correct relationship, and correct function." Then there are kong-ans where seemingly you can't do anything, but one clear action is required. And then there are kong-ans where you "just do it." There are kong-ans called "last-word" kong-ans, such as Duk Sahn carrying his bowls. The Nam Cheon cat kong-an teaches "moment-to-moment great love, great compassion, and the great bodhisattva way." This is a "love" kong-an that points to attaining unconditional love. The mouse kong-an is a "subject-like-this" kong-an, very simple, very easy.

Each of the ten chapters in this book, corresponding to the ten types of kong-ans, begins with a statement of the kong-an followed by Zen Master Seung Sahn's questions and commmentaries. Over the years he added two more gates, the eleventh and twelfth, to help deepen his students' wisdom.

Zen Master Seung Sahn used kong-ans to teach students correct situation, correct relationship, and correct function in their daily life. Here the kong-an is not so much a "test" as a technique to reveal how to live with wisdom and compassion. He called this his "Zen revolution," using the kong-an to teach us how to function in our everyday lives. As he says, "Do not think that the kong-an is separate from your life." It is not a rarefied or dry intellectual game played out in the interview room. Rather,

> [y]our kong-an practice and your daily life must connect. This is very important. Moment-to-moment correct situation, correct relationship, and correct function give rise to great love, great compassion, and the great bodhisattva way. So we use kong-an practice to make our everyday life correct. Then there is no difference between what we understand during interview time and the way we act in everyday life. Getting enlightenment is not special. Take away "opposites" thinking, become the absolute, and then there is no understanding, only wisdom! At that point, action and understanding have already become one.

Zen Master Seung Sahn was always a traveling Zen master. As a result, it was not always possible for his students to have personal meetings with him. He always encouraged them to write him about their problems and questions regarding practice. These letters grew into a voluminous correspondence, selections from which were then collected into "kong-an books." In residential Zen centers, a letter to Zen Master Seung Sahn and his reply are read as part of formal morning and evening Zen practice. These lively exchanges full of wit, pathos, cleverness, and arrogance—in short, the whole range of human experience—have served as the raw material for this book.

Kong-ans originate in the "before-thinking" mind, what Zen Master Seung Sahn called "don't-know mind." A clear response to a kong-an can only come from the same source, hence the reputed difficulty *and* the simplicity of kong-an training. If you are not thinking, the kong-an is no problem. But how can we reconnect to our before-thinking or don't-know mind? That is the point of Zen—finding our original self and allowing it to function to help our world. A good answer or a bad answer to the kong-an doesn't matter; an answer appears, an answer doesn't appear, it doesn't matter. What is important is keeping a don't-know mind moment to moment in your everyday life. Kong-an practice is a very powerful tool in this endeavor. The only way to attain it is to practice it; thinking won't help you.

However, if all this true, of what use is a book like this? Its genesis lies in what Zen Master Seung Sahn calls his students' "understanding sickness." We human beings suffer from our desire to rationalize and reduce our experience to something that will fit comfortably into our private world views. While it is the function of kong-ans to shatter our opinions, it is also necessary to treat understanding sickness with "understanding medicine." In a country such as Korea, which has an established Zen tradition, students are not accustomed to seeking, nor do they receive, elaborate explanations about kong-an practice. Students may encounter a Zen master, receive a kong-an, and practice it for years while having little or no contact with the teacher. After a lot of hard training, they again visit the master to test their minds. Here in the West, with our newly emerging Zen tradition, students have many questions, as well as strong opinions about practice. There is a tendency to rely on an outside authority in the form of a teacher, coupled with a real lack of information about kong-an practice—both what it is and how it is used. Hence this book.

As a teaching tool, kong-ans are an effective way for Zen teachers to check their students' attainment. The word *kong-an*, or "public case," refers to the Chinese custom of authenticating copies of public documents with a seal:

> If you have copies of a paper elsewhere, then you can compare the seals to check whether it is a true copy or not. So if someone says, "I have attained enlightenment," then the Zen master uses the kong-an to check whether that is true or not. He uses it to find out whether the student had correct understanding.

In the ongoing dialogue of kong-an practice, the teacher continually offers half of the public case and checks the authenticity of the student's half. In Zen Master Seung Sahn's words, "Your bodies are different, but your minds are the same." This face-to-face meeting in Zen dialogue is sometimes called "Dharma combat." In the following excerpt Zen Master Seung Sahn explains Dharma combat and how he has adapted it to teach kong-ans through letters. The student is checked on two things: clear mind (meditation energy) and wisdom (cognition).

First clear mind is checked:

> Korean Dharma combat style is like swordsmen fighting. A very high-class swordsman will, with his first attack, strike and completely kill his opponent. The next class of swords-

man must attack and strike two or three times before killing. A Zen master is like a sword master, always checking his student's mind by allowing space for attack. If the student's mind is not clear, then the master will strike and kill his student. But if the student is keen-eyed, he will attack in the space and with one blow strike the master dead.

For example:

Q: What is the way of Nam Cheon?
A (holding up a sickle): This sickle cost me thirty cents.
Q: I didn't ask you about your sickle!

To this second question, the keen-eyed student would answer, "The dog runs after the bone," which means "You are attached to my words." Then the master would say, "Is this correct?" to which the student would respond, "A second offense is not permitted." The master would then say, "Oh, wonderful!" Both attacking and defending are very important. This style of checking the student's meditation energy allows no chance for thinking and is used in face-to-face interviews.

Second, the student's cognition is checked by using such kong-ans as "Nam Cheon Kills a Cat" or "Duk Sahn Carrying His Bowls." The student is given the kong-an repeatedly and is allowed time to respond. Answers show the student's wisdom and whether he or she has attained the correct situation. Thus it is possible to be accurately checked in letters. For example:

1. The mouse eats cat food, but the cat bowl is broken. What does this mean? (the Tenth Gate)
2. One man makes a sword sound, another takes out a handkerchief, and another man waves his hands. What does this mean? (the Twelfth Gate)

In Korean style, attack and defense in these kong-ans is not necessary. Only one word or action is very important.

The basic requirement for undertaking kong-an practice is an attitude Zen Master Seung Sahn calls "try-mind," something a teacher can point out but not create in a student. It is the mind that refuses to quit, that comes back to try again even after mistakes, obstacles, and discouragement appear. Only through such trying can students come to believe in themselves completely. Without that sort of independence, simply understanding kong-ans is not enough.

You may understand that the sky is blue, but how much do you believe in that? That is important. If I ask you, "Why is the sky blue?" then what? If your mind is clear, then a correct answer can appear. "The sky is blue" must become yours! The understanding of a kong-an must become yours! Then you have wisdom.

There is perhaps an inevitable tendency for students to turn kong-an practice into something special, mysterious, or competitive. Actually, it is nothing special: a tool we can use—or a tool that uses us!—changing us in ways we can't foresee. Most important is not attaching to the kong-an. As Zen Master Seung Sahn says, we must "use kong-ans to take away our opinions. Don't attach to kong-an practice! Don't make it special. OK?"

A special thanks to Stanley Lombardo and Dennis Duremeier who prepared the first edition of this book.

Ten Gates

Open the gate—
All Buddhas and Bodhisattvas,
All human beings and animals,
All hungry ghosts and demons,
All together dancing.

Close the gate—
All things high and low,
Big and small, holy and unholy,
Disappear, disappear.
Cannot find anything.

Good and bad gate,
Dragon and snake gate,
Heaven and hell gate,
Appearing and disappearing gate,
Nirvana and Enlightenment gate.

KATZ and HIT gate,
Smile and one finger gate,
Stone dancing girl gate,
Snow fire gate,
Demon holding Buddha's baby gate,

Joju's "Mu" and four gates,
Three pounds of flax gate,

Nam Cheon kills the cate gate,
Duk Sahn carries his bowls gate,
Dropping ashes on Buddha gate,

Zen Master To Sol's three gates:
Where is your true nature now?
How then will he be reborn?
When the four elements disperse, where do you go?
Open your mouth, lose your tongue.

Zen Master Ko Bong's three gates:
Why does a cloud obscure the sun?
How can you not step on your shadow?
How can you escape being burned?
Holding your body, already you are dead.

Originally, there is nothing.
How do you open and close?
The mouse eats catfood but the cat bowl is broken.
DO!*
Through the gates—north south, east west.

—*Zen Master Seung Sahn*
Providence Zen Center
August 2, 1980

---

*Path.

Ten Gates

FIRST GATE
JoJu's Dog

*Someone asked JoJu Zen Master, "Does a
dog have buddha-nature?"
JoJu said, "Mu." ("No.")*

The first question is: Buddha said all things have buddha-nature.
Nature means substance. All things have this substance. But JoJu
said a dog had no buddha-nature. Which one is correct?

The second question is: JoJu said, "Mu." What does *mu* mean?
This *mu* has no meaning. If you find a meaning, that's a big mistake. If you are attached to yes and no, you will have a problem. Mu
is behind yes and no. Behind yes and no means behind everything.
Our world is an opposites world—heaven, earth; yes, no; man,
woman; good, bad—what is not opposites? But who made these
opposites? God, Buddha, human beings? We make opposites. If
you put it all down, return to before thinking, then there are no
opposites. If you have no opposites then mu is alive. If you have
opposites thinking, then mu hits you. JoJu said, "Mu," so this
monk is very surprised.

The third question is: Does a dog have buddha-nature? What
can you do? Many students understand this, but understanding
cannot help. You must attain the correct function of freedom from
life and death—only understanding freedom from life and death
cannot help you.

Dear Soen Sa Nim,

How are you?

Thank you for the letter you sent me. Also, thanks for the kong-an "JoJu's Dog." I have played (wrestled) with this kong-an for days, but I feel ready to reply to you:

> You ask who is correct, JoJu or Buddha?
> Buddha's finger points to moon
> JoJu's finger points at moon.
> Same moon, different finger.
> You ask what "Mu!" means.
> "Mu!" is JoJu's bark, "Mu!"
> You ask if a dog has buddha-nature.
> Dogs and men are just like this.
> When hungry they must eat, when tired
> they must sleep.
> AAAGH!

Well, I hope I have done well; if not, you must have a long stick to hit me in Alabama! I enjoy kong-ans and would like to continue my practice more with you. So until then, good-bye and thanks.

Ned

Dear Ned,

Thank you for your letter. How are you? I have just returned to Providence Zen Center.

About your dog kong-an: Your answers are not good, not bad. But first, Buddha and JoJu: Which one is correct? You say, "Buddha's finger points at the moon." JoJu's finger points at the moon. Same moon, different fingers." You are making many fingers. Also, you are attached to these fingers. How do you see the moon? So I say to you, your answer is like hitting the moon with a stick.

Next, you say JoJu's Mu means JoJu's bark, Mu! Why make JoJu's bark? I want *your* bark. I say to you, you are scratching your right foot when your left foot itches.

Next, you say, "Dogs and men are just like this. When hungry they must eat; when tired they must sleep." You say, "Just like this." But your speech is "only like this." Just like this and only like this are very different. Example: Here is a bell. If you say it is a bell, you are attached to name and form. If you say it is not a bell, you are attached to emptiness. So what is it? At that time, if you say, "When hungry, eat; when tired, sleep," or "The sky is blue, the tree is green," these are "only like this." They are only the truth, but they are not correct answers. At that time, you must pick up the bell and ring it. That is just like this. So just like this and only like this are different. Again I ask you, "Does a dog have buddha-nature?" Tell me! Tell me! If you don't understand, only go straight. Don't be attached to your understanding. Your understanding cannot help you. The true way is not dependent on understanding or not understanding. Only go straight, don't know. Then your opinion, your condition, and your situation will disappear, and the correct opinion, correct condition, and correct situation will appear. Then you are complete. OK?

I hope you only go straight, don't know, which is clear like space, soon finish the great work of life and death, get enlightenment, and save all people from suffering.

Yours in the Dharma,

S.S.

Dear Soen Sa Nim,

It is March 8. A gray mist surrounds my house and soaks the air. Monday, your letter came and hit me like a brick. You say I make "gates" (last letter) and "fingers" and "hindrances." I think this is so. I must make many things. I feel like I am attached to my thoughts and chase them (like a dog after its own tail). You say my answers are "not good, not bad." Thanks, I needed that!

About my dog kong-an: Does a dog have buddha-nature?

My answer is "I think so."

You say you hope I will only go straight and don't know. I will try.

I hope the Zen Center is doing well, and so are you. Thanks for writing me; I enjoy your letters very much. It is exciting to find my mistakes.

Respectfully yours,

Ned

Dear Ned,

Thank you for your wonderful letter. How are you?

Your mind is very smooth. Your only problem is that you are holding your understanding. Don't check your understanding. When your understanding disappears, then your mind is clear like space. If it is clear like space, it is like a clear mirror. Red comes, red; white comes, white. If somebody is sad, I am sad; if somebody is happy, I am happy. You can see; you can hear; you can smell; all, just like this, is truth.

Your answer to the dog kong-an was "I think so!" So I hit you thirty times. Why think? Zen is cutting off all thinking and becoming empty mind. Then this empty mind shines on everything; then everything is clear. The sky is blue, the trees are green.

The questions are:

1. Buddha said all things have buddha-nature. JoJu said the dog has no buddha-nature. Which one is correct?
2. Next, JoJu said, "Mu!" What does that mean?
3. I ask you, does a dog have buddha-nature?

Three questions. If you don't understand, only go straight. Don't check your understanding. If you are attached to understanding, you have a problem. Put it all down. Only don't know, always, everywhere. Don't worry about thoughts coming and going. Let it be. Try, try, don't know for ten thousand years nonstop. OK?

I hope you will only keep don't know, which is clear like space, soon finish the great work of life and death, get enlightenment, and save all people from suffering.

Yours in the Dharma,

S.S.

Dear Soen Sa Nim,

Thank you for your dog/master letter. How are you?

In this letter, you asked me about JoJu's dog. If I were JoJu, I could have considered cutting that monk up into little pieces, although he's hardly worth the effort. Some people mistake JoJu's answer and say, "JoJu said that a dog does not have buddha-nature." This, as Yuan Wu says, is like adding frost to the snow. Just by opening his mouth, that poor monk had already dropped into hell; JoJu just didn't want to follow him there. So using his mind-sword, JoJu said, "Mu!" and stopped that hell-bound train before it was too late.

Now, if you ask me this question—"Does a dog have buddha-nature?"—I might chase my tail around and around looking for an answer, but you know a dog chasing its tail has motion but no direction.

Yours in the Dharma,

Mark

Dear Mark,

Thank you for your letter. How are you? Happy New Year.

Your dog letter is not good, not bad, but much thinking, thinking, thinking. I hit you thirty times!! Again I ask you: A monk once asked JoJu, "Does a dog have buddha-nature? JoJu answered, 'Mu!'

1. Buddha said everything has buddha-nature. JoJu said a dog has no buddha-nature. Which is correct?
2. JoJu said, "Mu!" What does this mean?
3. Does a dog have buddha-nature?

You must answer these three questions. A lot of thinking is no good; you must believe in yourself 100 percent. Many words are not necessary . . . just one point, OK? If you don't understand, only go straight, don't know. Don't make anything; don't hold anything; don't check anything.

I hope you only go straight, don't know, which is clear like space, soon finish the great work of life and death, get enlightenment, and save all people from suffering.

Yours in the Dharma,

S.S.

6

SECOND GATE
JoJu's Washing the Bowls

*A monk once asked JoJu, "I have just entered
the monastery. Please teach me, Master."
JoJu said, "Did you have breakfast?"
"Yes," replied the monk.
"Then," said JoJu, "wash your bowls."
The monk was enlightened.*

What did the monk attain? This is very simple. "Please teach me."
"Did you have breakfast?" "Yes." "Then wash your bowls." That's
correct function, correct relationship. That is everyday mind. This
is an everyday-mind kong-an. Just do it. Everyday life is the truth
and the correct way. Everyday life is the great bodhisattva way.

The Second Gate kong-an is a just-like-this kong-an (see the
following letters). What did the monk attain? Don't attach to the
Zen master's speech. If you attain that point, you understand correct situation, correct function, and correct relationship moment
to moment. This monk attained his correct situation.

Dear Soen Sa Nim,

Thank you for your letter of July 8. You ask me, "What did the
monk attain when JoJu told him to wash his bowls?" I don't know

7

what the monk attained. I have never been to Paris, but I hear that it is a beautiful city.

> The sky was empty before creation,
> The sky is empty in creation;
> Creation is not there in the secret,
> Creation is not there in the manifest.
> The head is painful when hit by a stick,
> The stick is empty.

Will you please explain what you mean by the word *Dharma* when you use it at the end of your letters?

Respectfully with love,

Norm

———————————

Dear Norm,

Thank you for your letter. How are you?

You don't understand this kong-an. If you understand it correctly, you are already a great Zen master. If you "cannot," you cannot. If you say, "I can," you can. This can-mind means try, try-mind. If you don't understand the kong-an, you must only go straight— try, try, try, moment to moment, for ten thousand years nonstop. A good answer will then appear by itself. Good answers and bad answers don't matter. Here is a hint: Zen mind is not special. Everyday mind is Zen mind. Everyday mind means when-you-are-doing-something-you-must-do-it mind. When you are hungry, what? When you are tired, what? You already understand. That is Zen mind. Its name is "don't know"; its name is try-mind.

If you understand, you understand this kong-an. So I ask you one more time: JoJu Zen Master said, "Did you have breakfast?"

"Yes."

"Then wash your bowls."

When he heard this, the monk got enlightenment. What did the monk attain? Very easy. Don't think. Only just like this.

Your poem was wonderful. You are very attached to empty. I ask you, "What is empty?" Tell me! Tell me! If you open your mouth, I will hit you thirty times.

Next, you ask me, "What is Dharma?" How many eyes do you have? You can answer this. This is Dharma. Do you understand? If you don't understand, only go straight, don't know. Try, try, try for ten thousand years nonstop.

I hope you only go straight, don't know, which is clear like space, soon finish the great work of life and death, get enlightenment, and save all people from suffering.

Yours in the Dharma,

S.S.

Dear Soen Sa Nim

Welcome home from Europe.

I hope you enjoyed yourself and enlightened many people.

The newsletter said Zen Center has a new home. This is great. Maybe one day I can come visit you there and leave my "pen-zen" behind.

Eighty-four thousand thank-yous for my homework, "JoJu's Washing the Bowls"! As to what the monk attained,

> Don't know has no-answer
> with Nothing to Attain
> only a clean bowl.
> KATZ.

I also hope we will meet someday. Your teaching is wonderful, and I always look forward to your letters and poems. Your hit is fantastic!

> Rain falls on dry land
> Soaking innumerable Buddhas
> To the Bone.

Thank you,

Ned

Dear Ned,

Thank you for your letter. The answer is a little late because I just returned from Europe and have been quite busy.

About your kong-an answer: not good, not bad. Your head is a dragon but your tail is a snake. Also, this snake has legs. Many unnecessary words appear. Here are four kinds of "like this." You must understand these four kinds of like this:

1. Without like this. True emptiness. Silence. Complete stillness.
2. Become-one like this. True nature. KATZ! Hit, etc.
3. Only like this. The meaning is truth. Spring comes, the grass grows by itself. Three times three equals nine, etc.
4. Just like this. Just doing is truth. Go drink tea, wash your bowls, etc. For this kong-an, a just-like-this answer is necessary. If you speak a lot, you lose your tongue! Be careful! Again I ask you, "What did the monk attain?"

If you don't understand, only go straight, don't know for ten thousand years. Try, try, try, nonstop, OK?

I hope you only go straight, don't know, which is clear like space, soon finish the great work of life and death, get enlightenment, and save all people from suffering.

Yours in the Dharma,

S.S.

Dear Soen Sa Nim,

How are you doing, and how has your summer been?

In your last letter from Tahl Mah Sah, you asked me again what did JoJu's monk friend with the unwashed bowls attain after seeing the old master. I gave you a 90 percent answer, and the kong-an bomb did not explode.

What did the monk attain?

Bowl.

This is a feeble shot in the dark, of course, but I hope to soon be emptied of answers. I have not been able to put all of the time and effort into your kong-an that I previously intended, due to the fact that I have been using much of my free time to study electronics, in hope of getting a good job. I have approached my electronics study as a Zen discipline, however, and am mastering it with single-minded zeal and directness. Yet within me there is a need to get back to the kong-an and settle this matter. I wish to give all sentient beings the aid that only a patriarch can give.

Too many words!

Yours in the Dharma,

Dale

Dear Dale,

Thank you for your letter.

Your previous kong-an answer had much energy, but this answer has no energy. What's the matter with you? You must believe in yourself 100 percent, and moment to moment, you must keep your correct situation. The name for this is clear mind; the name for this is don't know. What are you doing now? When you do something, you must *do* it. That is your correct situation, clear mind, and don't know. You think the kong-an is over there; my life is here; my job is there. The kong-an, don't-know mind, clear mind, your job, your situation, your life: let them become one. Just now, what are you doing?

You said, "I have no time, so I can't work on the kong-an." This is very bad speech. The kong-an is your life; the kong-an is your just-now situation. Don't check your mind; don't check your feelings. Any kong-an is the correct situation for that time. Every day, everywhere, when you keep your correct situation moment to moment, any kong-an is not a problem.

You said that you are now studying electronics. This is Zen. You are correct. Electrical energy can change into anything. Sometimes it makes things hot, sometimes cold, sometimes makes wind, sometimes light, sometimes the correct time, sometimes food. This original energy has no name, no form. This energy is like our mind. If you correctly understand one kind of electrical form, then you correctly understand electricity's substance. You see a light. Where does this light come from? Light is electrical energy; electrical energy is light. Therefore, your moment-to-moment correct action is your true self, clear mind, and truth. An eminent teacher said, "Everyday mind is Zen mind and the truth." If you learn the correct way from electricity, then any kong-an is no problem.

Next, your answer: "Bowl." Your answer is like a blind man who wants to open the door and has just grabbed the doorknob. You must open the door. How do you do this? If you open your eyes, it is very easy. If you are still blind, it is very difficult. You must believe in your answer 100 percent. Then your eyes will open, and you will pass through the true door without any problem.

I hope you only go straight, soon open your eyes and pass through the true door, get enlightenment, and save all people from suffering.

Yours in the Dharma,

S.S.

Dear Soen Sa Nim,

That monk attained this.

Thank you for your letter. You are a very perceptive and encouraging old lion, and I look forward to meeting you next spring.

Zen is Zen; practice is practice. How could I speak of things going well or poorly? In the morning, breakfast, and after work, supper. Just this.

Take care. I promise to go straight and save all beings. Thank you for your great concern.

Yours in the Dharma,

Dale

Dear Dale,

Thank you for your letter. How are you and Linda? Happy New Year.

Your kong-an answer is "That monk attained this." What is *this*? I hit you thirty times. Your answer is like this: Here are some sweet things, many different kinds—honey, banana, sugar, apples. But you only say, "Sweet." What kind of sweet? You only say, "This." What is *this*?

Zen is Zen; practice is practice. This means understanding sweet, but what kind of sweet? What is Zen? What is practicing? Understanding cannot help you. You must taste correctly. Then you will attain banana sweet, sugar sweet, honey sweet, apple sweet. OK?

I hope you only go straight, don't know, soon finish the great work of life and death, get enlightenment, and save all people from suffering.

Yours in the Dharma,

S.S.

Dear Soen Sa Nim,

Thank you for your compassionate letter! How are you? I have read about the vast program for summer and fall, and I hope you are in good health!

I'm OK.

You gave me a kong-an, "JoJu's Washing the Bowls," and I answer:

Enclosed in your letter, I find your poem. You are very fast! Thank you for that!

I hope you are going on fine with spreading Buddhism. Good luck with the new Dharma room!

Gratefully,
Yours in the Dharma!

Bjorn

Dear Bjorn,

Thank you for your letter. How are you?

Your answer is very, very wonderful. That name is don't know. That name is mind. That name is Buddha and God and truth and absolute and complete and consciousness and everything. But you already understand, that is no name, no form, no speech. If you open your mouth, it is already a mistake. So you only send blank paper. But if you are attached to this mind, you are blankness. You must make that point function. If you don't understand, only go straight, don't know. Try, try, try for ten thousand years nonstop. OK?

I hope you only go straight, don't know, which is clear like space, soon finish the kong-an, get enlightenment, and save all people from suffering.

Yours in the Dharma,

S.S.

Most Venerable Zen Master,

In all reverence and compassion, thank you for informing me about the summer and fall retreats.

If you can see what I cannot see, if I can see what you cannot see—this is the blindness of bondage and karma.

In your letters, you always asked, "Is it the same or different?" You keep spitting mud at me from both sides of your mouth, and I'm very sorry that you suffer from splitting headaches. You should go to the place where there is neither sameness nor difference.

Self-reliance has been my only teacher, and experience is my only guide. I have not practiced, but every day I sweep away dust.

I have no robe, but each day I meditate continuously on work, troubles, and play. I have no attainment, but I come and go freely, and I differentiate the one and the many—like one gunman facing another.

The ancient Tang masters have "taught" me to reject anything that comes from words and practice, but especially to avoid attaching to their words and to avoid imitating them. I accept their words literally, without explanations or interpretation. They have given me the "cutting tools" of no-thought, no-form, and no-abode to help me keep away from attachments, keep away from separations, and in particular, keep away from keeping away.

I don't want frozen or muddied Zen. I don't want imitative, systematic, or gradual Zen. I don't "whip carts," and I don't imitate Buddha.

Without my living presence, I must humbly apologize to you for this letter, which is filled with egotistic claims and implications—all dead words and deadlier distinctions.

If you are not in peace, it's because you're in pieces.

Happy being!

> Yours in neither Doctrine
> nor No-Doctrine
>
> Tony

> Yesterday's shadows life
> and dawn uncovers all the roses—
> dewdrop falling
>
> (my own Haiku)

Dear Tony,

Thank you for your letter. How are you?

You have "I" and checking. These are not necessary. Don't make I. Don't make checking.

You understand too much. Understanding cannot help you. You say, "I do this, I do that, I do that." Is that necessary? If you have no I, then there is no problem. No hindrance means complete freedom—in other words, great love, great compassion, and the great bodhisattva way.

Zen means not making anything. Then moment to moment, you can keep your correct situation, correct function, and correct relationship. That is Zen. Here is a kong-an for you.

A monk once asked JoJu, "I have just entered the monastery. Please teach me, Master."

JoJu said, "Have you had breakfast?"

"Yes, I have," replied the monk.

"Then," said JoJu, "wash the bowls."

The monk was enlightened.

I ask you, "What did the monk attain?" If you attain this, you attain correct Zen. If you don't understand, only go straight, don't know. Don't make anything, don't check anything.

I hope you only go straight, don't know, which is clear like space, soon finish the great work of life and death, get enlightenment, and save all people from suffering.

Yours in the Dharma,

S.S.

Seong Am Calls Master

*Seong Am Zen Master would sit every day
in the Dharma room facing the blue
mountain. He used to call to himself every
day, "Master!" and would answer, "Yes?"*
   "You must keep clear!"
   "Yes!"
   *"Never be deceived by others, any day,
any time!"*
   "Yes! Yes!"

Seong Am used to call to himself and answer himself—two minds. Which one is the correct master?

Some people have not only two minds, but three minds, four minds, five minds, eighty minds; many, many minds—pain mind, sad mind, sex mind, money mind, all kinds of mind. Seong Am has only two minds: "Master!" "Yes!" "Keep a clear mind!" Two minds. Which one is the correct master? Two minds become one. If you become one, there is no mind, no master. Then you attain your true master. This is very important. To attain this, first your master and your mind must disappear; then you are nothing. If you are nothing, then your eyes, ears, nose, tongue, and body can work correctly and you can see your master—everything is your master.

Dear Soen Sa Nim,

Thank you for your last letter, which I have purposely delayed in answering. Today is a good day for answering letters.

Looking out the window, the fields multishaded greens, trees, and breeze. Horses, autos, and even a railroad car. Water forming a circle from an irrigation system, the sun glistening on the droplets. A man walking carefully to avoid rocks on the pathway. How wonderful it is!

You say, "Primary point is before thinking." And so it is! Who is the correct master? It matters not.

My mother, sister, and niece came to visit last month. We had a wonderful time.

The volcano erupted again, spewing ash and sulfur dioxide all over the place. No one seems to know when it will erupt again or if it might stop altogether. The air seems hazy all the time since it started, and the farmers have had problems.

There is a good chance for me to go on what is called "work release." That means I would be working during days, and spending evenings at the work release center. I would like very much to finish the BA degree I previously was working toward. I have about one and a half years left. The VA [Veteran's Administration] would help pay for tuition and the rest. I spent a little over seven years in the service (three in Vietnam).

> Thank you very much for caring,
> Sincerity, love, and sharing;
> This life is but a tool,
> and "I" the biggest fool.

> Yours in the Dharma,
> Gary

Dear Gary,

Thank you for your letter. How are you?

You describe what you see looking out of the window, talk about leaving prison on work release and going to a beautiful area, and going back to finish your BA degree. That is very wonderful.

In answer to "Seong Am Calls Master," you say, "It matters not." That is your idea. If you find Seong Am's correct master, then you can find your master and the universal master. Your saying it doesn't matter means my life doesn't matter; the universe doesn't matter; if this world is destroyed and disappears, it doesn't matter; also, if all people die, it doesn't matter. Doesn't matter is a very dangerous state of mind. It's also I-my-me mind.

So you must find Seong Am's master. Then helping other people is possible and world peace is possible. This is called correct direction, truth, and correct life—great love, great compassion, and the great bodhisattva way. I ask you again: Seong Am called himself, answered himself—two minds. Which is the correct master? Tell me, tell me! If you don't understand, only go straight, don't know. Try, try, try for ten thousand years nonstop, OK?

I hope you only go straight, don't know, which is clear like space, soon finish the great work of life and death, and save all people from suffering.

Yours in the Dharma,

S.S.

Dear Soen Sa Nim,

Once again my karma has decreed that I can't be with you. The illness of my wife made it necessary for me to return home. My question that cannot be asked will be my practice until I see you again in July.

I have been going to a Raja-Yoga center near my home. The guru-ji uses "word medicine," which tastes a little strange, but in the stomach, it's all the same.

In my interview, you asked me to show you the true master. My answer is, don't be deceived!

Bob

Dear Bob,

Thank you for your letter. How are you and your wife?

I know you are a busy man. Coming to the Zen Center, not coming to the Zen Center, seeing me or not seeing me doesn't matter. Moment to moment, how do you keep just-now mind? How much do you believe in yourself? That is very important. Always keep a clear mind, then you'll always have enough. Moment to moment, you must keep your correct situation.

You visited a yoga center and said that the taste is different, but in your stomach, it's the same. This means your practicing is correct. If your stomach has enough, then there is no problem.

Regarding your answer to the correct master kong-an: "Don't be deceived!" is not the correct master. At the primary point, there is no master, no you, no I, nothing at all. Then the correct, just-like-this master can appear. "Don't be deceived" is not a bull's-eye answer. Give me another answer, OK?

I hope you always keep a mind that is clear like space, soon finish the great work of life and death, get enlightenment, and save all people from suffering.

Yours in the Dharma,

S.S.

Dear Soen Sa Nim,

Thank you for your letter. All is "enough" with my family and me.

My answer to the correct master kong-an is: "(He is) writing this letter."

Bob

Dear Bob,

Thank you for your letter. How are you and your family?

You said all is "enough": that is wonderful.

To the correct master kong-an, you said, "writing this letter." That is *your* master. What is just-like-this master?

I hope that you always keep don't-know mind, soon finish your homework, become a great man, and save all people from suffering.

Yours in the Dharma,

S.S.

Dear Soen Sa Nim,

Thank you for your letter. I hope you are well, and I hope that your trip to Korea went well.

However, the bone of space suddenly appears, crashing Seong Am's skull and smashing "What are you?" to smithereens. What can you do?

Put down "wonderful." Put down "hit thirty times." Put down "don't-know mind."

Don't you know by now that a wooden typewriter clacks without keys?

See you soon,

Steve

Dear Steve,

Thank you for your letter. How are you?

Your letter is not good, not bad. I ask you: Seong Am Zen Master called himself and answered himself—two minds. Which one is the correct master?

Your typewriter said, "You are scratching your right foot when your left foot itches."

You misunderstand the four kinds of "like this": without like this, become-one like this, only like this, and just like this. If you are clear about these four kinds of like this, you can understand your mistake. If you don't understand your mistake, you don't understand the four kinds of like this and your true self, which means you don't understand your master. How do you know Seong Am's master?

I hope you go straight, don't know, which is clear like space, soon find Seong Am's master and your master, get enlightenment, and save all people from suffering.

Yours in the Dharma,

S.S.

Dear Soen Sa Nim,

Arrived here only a few weeks ago from a five-day visit with Seo Un Su Nim and a seven-day *sesshin* with Maezumi Roshi. Other than that, I really don't have anything much to say for myself, nothing to "show you" in the Zen sense.

Seo Un was so very kind to me in every way. I am very grateful I was able to have that time with him. He is such a good and strong Dharma friend.

The sesshin was, in many respects, the strongest I've ever sat. The strain and pain were sometimes tough, but "something" proved to be even tougher, more durable. What is that something?

During the sesshin, I had what (for me) was a new experience. That is, during some of the sittings, I had what I can only describe as "blank spaces." I would "come to" and find myself sitting there with no recollection of periods of time or of any activity that might have gone on around me. I don't know if that went on for seconds, minutes, or what—a kind of periodic amnesia.

I asked, "What is that 'something.' Also, what is that which asks? What is that which determines to keep going, trying?"

I still have no Zen answers to the kong-ans you gave me. The monk of two minds is a very ordinary situation. Two minds: one speaking, one answering. How can that be? In my own mind, is not to speak also to answer? Please, Soen Sa Nim, give me a clue! Okay, so send me thirty blows, there is a lot of love in that too!

I want so very much to solve this kong-an. I feel really ashamed of the "garbage" I just wrote. Stay with me, and I promise I'll give you a wonderful answer one of these letters!

Hope to hear from you soon.

Gassho,

Virginia (Zui Shin)

Dear Virginia,

Thank you for your letter. How are you?

You said in your letter that you had a five-day visit with Seo Un Su Nim and a seven-day sesshin with Maezumi Roshi. That is wonderful.

When you sit, sometimes you have blank space. This is called lost mind. There are three kinds of mind: lost mind, one mind, and clear mind. Lost mind is when everything is lost; no eyes, no ears, no nose, no tongue, no body, no mind, no perceptions, no consciousness—so no direction, nothing at all. In Korean, this is called *rak gong*. *Rak* means "fall into," and *gong* means "empty." At that time, your don't-know mind is not clear. Already you lose your don't-know mind. If you lose your don't-know mind, you lose your correct situation.

What is correct situation?

When you are hungry, just eating is the correct situation. When you drive, just drive—red light comes, stop; green light comes, go—that is the correct situation. When it is sitting time, what is the correct situation? You must find what is the correct situation when you sit . . . what is correct sitting?

Next, you ask, "What is that 'something'?" If you make something, you have something, but that something will kill you! I say, "Don't make something, don't hold something, don't be attached to something." Then you are complete. If you open your mouth, again you make something, and I will hit you thirty times!

Regarding your kong-an. You say, "In my own mind, is not to speak also to answer?" If you use this style, already you lose your tongue! This kind of thinking is a bad habit.

You already understand our style. If you want something, my Zen stick will hit you. Be very careful!

Only go straight, don't know, always and everywhere—for ten thousand years nonstop. Try, try, try!

One drop of water is stronger than a rock, because if it steadily drips on the same point, it will eventually make a hole.

I hope you only go straight, don't know, which is clear like space, soon finish the great work of life and death, get enlightenment, and save all people from suffering.

Yours in the Dharma,

S.S.

Dear Soen Sa Nim,

Did you have a wonderful trip, and are you well? I hope so! And thank you for your letter of September 8—which actually disappointed me a bit because my answer to Seong Am's master was the flower painting. Before your letter arrived, the photo of you came, sent by Louise. On receiving the photo of you sailing, I took this for the answer to my answer and was happy.

Then your letter came which said I had opened my mouth; but in reality, I had not opened my mouth. I was quoting your previous letter in which you said, "If you say the same, I hit you thirty times; if you say different, I hit you thirty times." So I wrote, "If I can't make a gesture, or a silence, because I am here, I will send you my answer under separate cover. My answer was the flower, which was my gesture. Is it still wrong? I feel it is right. But one can't differ with a Zen master, can one? Or can one?

As always, Soen Sa Nim, thank you, and I send you all my best wishes in the Dharma.

Elizabeth

Dear Elizabeth,

Thank you for your letter.

You said that the flower painting was actually the answer to the "Seong Am Calls Master" kong-an. Now I understand! But I did not ask for a flower! Seong Am calls himself, answers himself, which one is the correct master? Only flower is not enough, even though the flower is very beautiful! Give me a beautiful "your master"! If you think flower is master, master is flower, then I hit you! Flower is only flower; master is only master! OK?

I hope you only go straight ("What am I?") and keep a don't-know mind, which is clear like space, soon finish the great work of life and death, get enlightenment, and save all people from suffering.

Yours in the Dharma,

S.S.

Bodhidharma Has No Beard

Hok Am Zen Master said, "Why does Bodhidharma have no beard?"

First question: What is Bodhidharma's original face?

Next: Why does Bodhidharma have no beard?

Everybody has seen Bodhidharma's picture, and he always has a big beard. We call this an attack kong-an. Here is an example: There is a very famous painter whom you want to draw your portrait. You are willing to pay him a lot of money to do this. "Please, will you draw me?" When he is finished with it, there is your portrait and . . . Look at that! No hair! It looks like a monk! You are very surprised. Why no hair? What can you do? You've paid a lot of money, and he is a famous painter. Maybe there is some meaning. At that point, what can you say to him? If your mind is clear, then no problem, just do it.

In the same way, we know Bodhidharma always has a beard. Then why does Hok Am Zen Master ask, "Why does Bodhidharma have no beard?" That, we say, is an attack kong-an. There are many kinds of attack kong-ans. Here's another example: You clean your body in the shower but where do you clean your mind? Where do the sun, the moon, and the stars come from? These are all attack kong-ans. So again I ask you, "Why does Bodhidharma have no beard?" Tell me! Quick, tell me!

Dear Soen Sa Nim,

Welcome back to America. I hope your trip was a good one. How are you feeling? We have all been concerned about your health because of the rigors of your trip. I think that Steve is a very good doctor and that you should listen to his advice about your health. All of us in New Haven have adopted him as our doctor! You should get much rest during the next few weeks because you have much important teaching to do in America, and we have much hard training to accomplish.

Thank you for your letter from Korea. Although I don't completely understand karma in a clear way, I'm doing Kwan Seum Bosal (repeating the name of the bodhisattva of compassion, using it as a mantra) when I'm between classes, cooking, driving to work, etc. Many aspects of karma (such as past lives) are somewhat difficult for Americans to comprehend. Our cultural background is so different from your own. I assume that all of these questions will disappear when attainment of like-this mind appears.

I have enclosed answers to kong-ans on a separate sheet. You asked me about Bodhidharma's not having a beard several months ago when we discussed attack kong-ans. I had not considered it since then, but as I was reading the *Mu Mun Kwan* the other evening, an answer came to me when I read that kong-an.

I have two questions: (1) After one attains just-like-this mind, what happens to the attainment if serious injury to the mind results from an accident (like an auto accident) or, even more likely in contemporary scientific culture, if "life" is prolonged by machine or drugs after the functioning mind becomes dormant. I ask this because such Buddhist teaching stresses keeping clear mind right up until death.

(2) My other question is a personal one. Since I last wrote to you, my stepfather has died, leaving my mother alone in Arizona (twenty-five hundred miles from here). I've invited my mother to come visit Marilyn and I during Christmas vacation because she will be lonesome and we haven't seen her in several years. My mother is a wonderful person and a very serious Christian Baptist. She is a great bodhisattva in many respects and has helped people throughout her life, even when it involved great self-sacrifice. However, she is not a highly educated person and has not been exposed as far as I know to any non-Western–based systems of teaching. I'm afraid that my Buddhist practice would upset her very much and she would not understand at all. If I were very strong, maybe I could teach her, but I don't know if my understanding is powerful enough. My practice has grown to the point where it permeates my total life, and I would not like to conceal this most important aspect of my being from her. Also, getting up and sitting with the group every morning is very important to me, as is a period of reading/sitting before bed in the evening. Do you have suggestions as to how I should approach this situation during my mother's visit (probably for about ten days)?

See you in two weeks for Yong Maeng Jong Jin [YMJJ].

Peace and love,

Bob

P.S. *Bodhidharma's Beard*
Why are you dragging up the carcass of Bodhidharma? Skeletons don't have beards!

Dear Bob,

Thank you for your letter. How are you and your family? It is very kind of you to be concerned about my health. Steve has introduced me to a very good diabetes specialist in Providence, and he has given me some new medicine. My body is stronger, so don't worry.

You say you don't completely understand karma. When you completely understand karma, you will understand life and death. If you completely understand life and death, then you will get freedom from life and death and you will become a great no-hindrance human being. So you must completely understand karma. Karma is a name; name is empty; so karma is made by thinking; and if you cut thinking, there is no karma. An eminent teacher said, "Without thinking, just like this is buddha-nature." Don't make many difficult aspects of karma, only go straight ahead with Kwan Seum Bosal. That is very important!

In answer to your first question: If you attain just like this, there is no death and no life, only infinite time and space. Then how can you worry about an automobile accident or your sick body in the hospital? The *Heart Sutra* says, "Perceive that all five skandhas are empty and be saved from all suffering and distress." Why do you worry? That perception means just-like-this mind. Put it all down. Don't check yourself.

As for your second question: I think your mother is a very good person. Christian and Buddhist bodhisattva action are not different. Don't be attached to name. If a person thinks, "I am a great bodhisattva and I help many people," then that person has lost the way. I don't think your mother is like that. Although she has little formal education, still her mind has a high education. In the true way, Eastern and Western religion are not different. The Bible says, in John 14:6, "I am the way, the truth, and the life . . ." There is no need to talk of Buddhism. Many people use the word *I*, but we must attain our big I. Teach her that we must cut through the mind that makes subject and object. Subject and object are only made by thinking. If you cut your thinking, there is no subject or object, and we will find the true way. I hope your good training will help your mother find enlightenment.

Your answer to Bodhidharma's beard kong-an is like the dog running after the bone, so I hit you! What can you do? I hope the next retreat you will give me a good answer.

Sincerely,

S.S.

———————————

Dear Soen Sa Nim,

How are you? Thank you for coming to this YMJJ with us and for teaching us.

We just finished a house meeting—a little noisy but everyone tried and everyone was involved.

You gave us a homework question: "Why does Bodhidharma have no beard?"

Here is my answer: Bodhidharma has no beard.

Also, I have a problem, about which maybe you can make some comment. At last Thursday night's Dharma talk, I asked you a question about the body's job. I understand a little, maybe, but I am still confused.

You say to first control the six senses. And then what? If I manage to control my six senses, is it possible then that my body's job will change? Is there a correct job and not-correct job? Can the body's job help other people as well as the original job? Or should

I keep my job no matter what it is because it pays my rent to live at the Zen Center?

Bobby is a nurse, George and Linc are carpenters, Dyan makes cushions, Colin teaches school, Anita makes beautiful instruments. These jobs seem to me to be helping other people. How can my job as an order clerk selling car repair manuals help other people? The books are overpriced, and the president of the company makes two hundred thousand dollars a year and squanders the money.

The idea I have about helping or not helping other people is not my only concern; also, I am bored at work. If I understand this boredom, a product of my uncontrolled sense, will the job make better sense? Will I see another job I should take? Maybe I should find another job, but I do not have faith that I could find a good one and do not understand what a good one is.

Again, thank you for
your teaching,

Anne

Dear Anne,

Thank you for your letter. How are you? This letter is a little late—I'm sorry. We have had a retreat and just finished a three-day *kido*. There were forty-two people, and everyone practiced hard and cleaned their minds.

Regarding your kong-an: You are attached to Bodhidharma's beard, so I hit you thirty times!

If you don't understand, only go straight, don't know. Thinking, thinking, thinking—this is the worst sickness.

You talked about your job. If you can control the six senses, then changing jobs is not necessary. Any job is OK if there is not like and dislike. Next, you talk about original job and body job. I ask you, "Are your original job and body job the same or different?" Tell me! Tell me! If you keep the correct situation moment to moment, then your body's job and your original job are never separate. So put I, my, me all down.

Don't check your mind, don't check your feelings, don't check your job, also don't check your company. If you check, you will have a problem. What are you doing now? That is most important. If you are checking, then many problems appear. Put it all down— your idea, your opinion, your condition, your situation. Then your job is your original job and the great bodhisattva job.

I hope you only go straight and don't know, which is clear like space, don't check anything, soon finish your homework, get enlightenment, and save all people from suffering.

Yours in the Dharma,

S.S.

Dear Soen Sa Nim,

How are you and the Los Angeles smog getting along? Very well, I am sure.

You say Zen is not difficult. The most complicated theory is very easy once you understand; but if you do not understand, it is very complicated. Is not Zen like this? Abstract ideas I find fairly easy to deal with—their emptiness is manifest. But feelings, impulses, perceptions, consciousness—all I can say is WOW! So I try and try and try and maybe someday soon . . . In this respect, it is very good living with Jim, who is a high-class student and helps my practice. But he has one big problem—how can he expect to attain Korean Enlightenment as long as he doesn't like kimchee?

One more thing. I am disturbed by the appearance that a lot of emphasis is placed on simply learning a different way of speaking about things—kind of a special language or philosophical system. That's OK in itself, but sometimes it begins to sound like a formula, and "direct pointing" becomes just two words. Two examples: When you talked about primary point in my last interview, and when you explained the four kinds of "like this" in your last Dharma talk at Berkeley. Please explain. (Well, so much for Bodhidharma's clean-shaven face.)

> Bodhidharma has no beard?
> I find that very weird!
> But yet, I find it commonplace
> That he has no face.

My warmest greetings to you and all the folks at Tahl Mah Sah.

> Sincerely,
>
> Eric

Dear Eric,

Thank you for your letter. How are you and Jim? Here in L.A. it is warmer than Berkeley, and 7 million people are living here. Have you been to Los Angeles? Maybe when you come to Los Angeles, the smog will kill you. What can you do?

You said, "The most complicated theory is very easy once you understand; but if you do not understand, it is very complicated. Is not Zen like this? Abstract ideas I find fairly easy to deal with—their emptiness is manifest." I ask you: You are a scientist. Heavy things appear, hit the ground hard. Light things appear, hit the ground lightly. Everything has weight. Does the earth have weight? How many pounds?

Also you are checking, checking, checking: "This is emptiness; this is no feeling, no perception, no consciousness; this is no impulse." Don't make emptiness, impulses, feeling, perception, or consciousness, OK? How you use these things is very important. Sometimes use emptiness; sometimes use impulses; sometimes feeling, perception, and consciousness. The name for this is freedom, the name for this is great love; the name for this is the great bodhisattva way. Why hold something? Why make something? Why attach to something? Put it all down. Only go straight, don't know for ten thousand years nonstop. Try, try, try, OK?

Do you know the universal formula? The name for it is truth; its name is nature; its name is your correct direction. I ask you, "What is the universal formula?" If you understand this universal formula then Zen, physics, psychology, art, literature, auto mechanics—all are no problem. Then your computer automatically reflects. The name for this is kong-an interview.

Here is a poem for you:

> Bodhidharma has no beard.
> Half-crazy.
> Bodhidharma has beard.
> Completely crazy.
> Bodhidharma has no face.
> Hit you thirty times.
> Bodhidharma never cut beard,
> Sat for nine years in Sorim.

I hope you only go straight, don't know, which is clear like space, soon finish the great work of life and death, get enlightenment, and save all people from suffering.

Yours in the Dharma,

S.S.

Hyang Eom's "Up a Tree"

*Master Hyang Eom said, "It is like a man
up a tree who is hanging from a branch by
his teeth; his hands cannot grasp a branch,
his feet cannot touch the tree—he is tied
and bound. Another man under the tree
asks him, 'Why did Bodhidharma come to
China?' If he does not answer, he evades
his duty and will be killed. If he answers,
he will lose his life."*

*Question: If you are in the tree, how
can you stay alive?*

You are hanging by your teeth, so you cannot open your mouth.
Also, you cannot move your hands, you cannot move your body,
you cannot do anything. This is a Kyung Chul Mun kong-an: everything is stopped, you cannot do anything. Only one thing is possible. What is that one thing? There is only one way, not two ways. If
you find that, then a good answer is possible. The man under the
tree asks you, "Why did Bodhidharma come to China?" If you open
your mouth to answer, you fall to your death. If you do not answer,
you evade your duty as a bodhisattva and will be killed. If you are
in the tree, how can you stay alive? That is the big question.

If you pass this gate, you have finished half of the kong-ans. We
have about 1,700 kong-ans. If you pass this gate, you have passed

the equivalent of 850 kong-ans. So this is a difficult kong-an. However, if you only understand this kong-an, it's not interesting. If it becomes *yours*—if you attain it—then your mind, your body, and your whole world become one and function correctly. At that time you attain freedom from life and death. So you must attain freedom from life and death, which means there is no life, no death. But if you hold on to that, you will have a problem.

Dear Venerable Seung Sahn,

I have been pondering the kong-an you gave me of the man who was hanging by his teeth from a tree, over a precipice, and under the tree another person asks him, "Why did Bodhidharma come from the West?"

I think the reply could be, who is hanging from the tree? Bodhidharma did not come from the West. No one is hanging from the tree.

Or a story that I thought of: A river is approaching a desert. It wishes to cross the desert, but every time it gets near, the water is absorbed by the sand. What can it do? A cloud approaches and lifts the water from the river into its folds, carries it safely across the desert, and drops it as rain on the other side.

The man hanging from the tree is the conceptual mind. There is no way he can reply to a question that comes from the mind. The only answer is transcending, in letting go of the conceptual and entering no-mind. That is why the question was never asked. That is why the river became a cloud.

Yours in the Dharma,

Jean

Dear Jean,

Thank you for your letter. How are you?

Your answer is not good, not bad. You already understand this kong-an. You are correct, but your speech is understanding; understanding is thinking. You must *attain* this kong-an.

In your answer you already opened your mouth, so you are already dead. What can you do? This kong-an already said, "If he doesn't answer, he evades his duty. If he does answer, he loses his life." He cannot use his hands, cannot use his feet, cannot use his mouth. If you are in the tree, what can you do? If you correctly understand this situation, then you understand.

You told a story about a river. You understand, but as I said, understanding is thinking. Thinking cannot help you. You say transcend. What is transcend? What is no mind? You must show me.

Someone asked Ma Jo Zen Master, "What is Buddha?"

He said, "Mind is Buddha. Buddha is mind."

The next day, another person asked him, "What is Buddha?"

He said, "No mind, no Buddha."

Which one is correct? Many words are not necessary. You must correctly understand just-now mind. Just-now mind is not dependent on words, not dependent on time and space, not dependent on life and death, not dependent on Buddha and God, not dependent on anything. Only depend on your true self. If you don't understand, only go straight, don't know. Don't check anything.

I hope you will go straight, don't know, soon finish your homework, get enlightenment, and save all people from suffering.

Yours in the Dharma,

S.S.

Dear Soen Sa Nim,

Hello. How are you? Thank you for your wonderful letter. So far away! Now I am in Kansas, in the middle of the country. Snow is falling, and I wonder what I am doing.

The other night, I was at a friend's house for dinner, and very late at night, when everyone had drunk too much and eaten too much and was very sleepy, he suddenly wanted to know about Zen. About satori. He thought that he had attained many books. But I was lost, on the far end of some dream. And then he showed me a magazine with interviews of three roshis. They were so simple and clear! I had forgotten. I keep forgetting. What is this that I'm doing?

There is a popular song by Paul Simon called "Slip Slidin' Away." That is how it is. Suddenly I realize that I am dreaming, but how did I slip into it?

Jeff S. tells me that the calligraphy of the Berkeley Zen Center says, "What is this?"

In Princeton, I fell in love. But I left him to work here. I think everything's OK, and then a song comes on the record player and suddenly there is nothing but grief. Now, writing this, just grief. What is this? All this moving here and there. Why? I am a mathematician, he is a physicist. What does this mean? Correct job, correct love, correct pain?

And then, boom, now mathematics time. Now teaching time. Now clean the house time. Boom, boom, boom, one after another. Easy to use these to cut off feeling. To live inside my fantasies, excuses, plans, rewards, punishments. What are they?

This man hanging from the branch by his teeth. You ask, "How can he stay alive?"

What is there to keep?
Hope you are well.

Love,

Judy

Dear Judy,

Thank you for your letter. How are you? Here in California, it is very warm; there are many flowers and blue mountains. I just finished a retreat in Berkeley and was thinking about you. Just at that time, I received your beautifully handwritten letter.

You said that you visited friends, ate and drank too much, slept and talked Zen too much, also got too much satori. Sometimes that's OK, but if you always do too much, you make too much karma, and that is very dangerous.

Your friend wants satori. He made satori, also he lost satori, which means this is *his* satori. You must tell him that attaining no satori is true satori. Don't make satori; don't make words; don't make feeling; don't make anything. Then everything is complete.

What are you doing now? Is it satori or not? If you say, "Satori," I hit you. What can you do? If you answer correctly, you have already graduated from satori. Satori is not special. You make special, so you have special, but this special is not satori and cannot help you.

You spoke of the song "Slip Slidin' Away," of the Berkeley Zen Center calligraphy, of love, and of grief. Also you said, "Now, writing this, just grief. What is this?" Then formally, you said, "...boom, now mathematics time. Now teaching time. Now clean the house time. Boom, boom, boom."

Why do you go around, around, around? What is your correct direction? If you have correct direction, then around, around, around is no problem. If you have no direction, then around, around, around is like a desire-dog. I want food, so around, around, around. Desire-dog is your karma; you must find your dog's master. That is very important.

You are a mathematician. Here is a poem for you:

$$9 \times 9 = 81$$
$$81 \times 0 = 0$$
$$10,000 \times 0 = 0$$
$$\text{Buddha} \times 0 = 0$$
$$\text{Everything} \times 0 = 0$$
$$0 = 81/0$$
$$0 = \text{Buddha}/0$$
$$0 = 0$$
$$\text{Buddha} = \text{Buddha}$$
$$81 = 9 \times 9$$

So, 0 makes everything; 0 is able to do everything, but who makes 0? Do you have 0? Tell me! Tell me! If you open your mouth, I hit you thirty times. If you close your mouth, I hit you thirty times. What can you do?

Your answer to the kong-an "Hyang Eom's 'Up a Tree'" is "What is there to keep?" You are already dead.

I hope you only go straight, don't know, which is clear like space, soon finish the great work of life and death, get enlightenment, and save all people from suffering.

Yours in the Dharma,

S.S.

Dear Soen Sa Nim,

It was good seeing you in New Haven last weekend at retreat. I'm glad you are feeling better now and that you are in such good form (as always, it seems)! I can now see why you spend time at different centers—students too attached to Zen master!

I feel I connected with your teaching last weekend as I never have before. It has taken a long time and much hard training to reach this point, though it is only a beginning (as each new realization always seems to be). Thank you.

I have answers for you to my homework:

From March, "Hyang Eom's 'Up a Tree'":

I hit you with Mount Sumeru before you open your mouth.

Since I will be taking the Precepts December 10, I look forward to seeing you then.

> Yours truly,
>
> Ralph

Dear Ralph,

Thank you for your letter. How are you and your family?

I was also glad to meet you at the New Haven Zen Center.

You said that the Zen master must go around and around. An around-and-around Zen master is not such a good Zen master. If you are a strong Zen master, you stay in one place; all people come to see you there. So I am a low-class Zen master.

Long ago, all great Zen students only met a great Zen master one time, then returned to their place—some people six years, some people eight years, some people ten years—only-go-straight mind. Then they got enlightenment, then visited the Zen master, got transmission, then became great Zen masters. But nowadays people want to see the Zen master very much, want to hear Dharma speeches, and want to have many interviews. If your great faith, great courage, and great question are strong, one time is enough. This means, if don't-know mind is strong, this don't-know mind is better than Zen masters, better than Buddha and God. I think you already met me one time, so this is enough. If you want more, you will become low class, OK? If you come and see me, you must bring me one word.

Next, your homework. You said, "I hit you with Mount Sumeru before you open your mouth." You already open your mouth, so you are already dead. What can you do? In this kong-an, you cannot speak, you cannot use your hands. Action and speech are not possible. You must answer me without your mouth, without action.

I hope you always only go straight, don't know, which is clear like space, soon finish the great work of life and death, and save all people from suffering.

Yours in the Dharma,

S.S.

Dear Soen Sa Nim,

Thank you for coming to Yong Maeng Jong Jin in New Haven.

"Hyang Eom's 'Up a Tree'"
How will he save his life?
There is no life for him to save.

Hyang Eom's "Up a Tree"

Only go straight, don't know.
It is raining outside.

> Sincerely,
> Paul

────────────────

Dear Paul,

Thank you for your letter. How are you?

Your homework answer is not good, not bad. But you said, "There is no life for *him*..." You are already dead. Again I ask you, "If *you* are in the tree, how can you stay alive?" Only go straight, don't know. That is correct. Outside, it is raining—this is also correct. Your answer is not correct. Next time, please give me a correct answer.

> Yours in the Dharma,
> S.S.

Dropping Ashes on the Buddha

*Somebody comes to the Zen Center smoking
a cigarette, blows smoke, and drops ashes
on the Buddha. If you are standing there at
the time, what can you do?*

This is a famous kong-an. Even many older students don't understand this kong-an. But if you only go straight, don't know, try, try, try, then it is possible to pass this gate. In this kong-an, the man smoking the cigarette thinks, "I already have enlightenment. I already am Buddha and Dharma and the true way." He is very attached to the idea that he has attained universal substance, that he has realized freedom from life and death. He thinks he has attained one point—no life, no death. But he still has a problem because he is attached to one point, attached to emptiness.

As an eminent teacher once said, "One by one, each thing is complete; one by one, each thing has it." For example, this is a stick. This stick's substance and your substance—are they the same substance? If you don't know, then I will explain. When you are thinking, your mind and my mind are different. When you cut off all your thinking, then your mind and my mind are the same. If you keep don't-know mind 100 percent—only go straight, don't know—then your don't-know mind, my don't-know mind, everybody's don't-know mind are all the same don't-know mind. This don't-know mind has already cut off all thinking, which means there is no thinking. No thinking is empty mind. Empty mind is before thinking. Your before-thinking mind is your substance; my before-thinking mind is my substance. Every human being's substance is the same substance. When you keep a don't-know mind 100 percent, then already you are the universe and the universe is you. You and everything are one. That is what we call primary point. So primary point's name is don't know. But primary point has been given many names. Some say primary point is mind, or Buddha, or enlightenment, or God, or nature, or substance, or absolute, or energy, or holiness, or consciousness. But true primary point is before thinking. Before thinking there is no speech, no word, so if I open my mouth about primary point, it's a mistake. In Zen we have a famous saying: "Opening your mouth is already a mistake." But if you keep don't-know mind 100 percent, then you and everything are already one.

So I ask you, if you keep a don't-know mind, this stick and you—are they the same or different?

Do you understand this point? If you are only attached to this point, there is no you, no I, no mind, no Buddha, nothing at all. So you think, "Ohhhh, I am already enlightened!" It is possible for you to come to the temple smoking a cigarette and drop ashes on the Buddha—no problem. But you don't understand your correct situation, correct relationship, correct function moment to moment. Everyday mind is Zen mind. This man has only attained freedom from life and death; he doesn't understand his correct function. One more step is necessary. When he is dropping ashes on the Buddha, at that moment what can you do? How can you teach him?

Dear Zen Master,

Answer to "Dropping of Ashes on Buddha" kong-an: Zen master fetches ashtray, sweeps ashes off Buddha into ashtray. Then bows to ashtray, bows to man, bows to Buddha.

Keeping don't-know or before-thinking mind, how then is it possible to sit Zen or bow to the Buddha? I never met Buddha, know nothing of enlightenment, so why bow? Why is Buddha special? Why wear robes?

There is no such thing as a mistake; there is only what happens. Is this correct understanding?

What is there to say?

Paul

Dear Paul,

Thank you for your letter. How are you?

Your "Dropping Ashes on the Buddha" kong-an answer is not good, not bad. But you are scratching your right foot when your left foot itches. Your answer misses the point. This is because the man already thinks, "I got Enlightenment; I am Buddha; I am Dharma." If you open your mouth or do any action, he will hit you, which means he is testing your mind. What can you do?

Our school has four kinds of "like this":

1. Without like this: True emptiness. Silence. Complete stillness.
2. Become-one like this: True nature. KATZ! Hit, etc.
3. Only like this: The meaning is truth. Spring comes, the grass grows by itself. Three times three equals nine, etc.
4. Just like this: Just doing is truth. Go drink tea, wash your bowls, etc.

Example. Here is a bell. If you say it is a bell, you are attached to name and form. If you say it is not a bell, you are attached to emptiness. Is this a bell or not? What can you do? At that time, a without-like-this answer is silence. If you shout, "KATZ!" or hit the floor, this is a become-one like-this answer. If you say, "The sky is blue, the grass is green," or "The bell is gold," this is only like this. What is a just-like-this answer? Pick up the bell and ring it.

This man only understands without like this and become-one like this. He doesn't understand only like this and just like this. How do you teach him only like this and just like this? How do you fix his mind? He is very attached to primary point, which means without like this and become-one like this.

Yours in the Dharma,

S.S.

Dear Soen Sa Nim,

Who am I?

Even before I took the Precepts last April, this question was with me, so much so that sometimes I think I am this question. When I get up in the morning, this question is in the mirror with me. When I get depressed, discouraged, or egotistical, this question pops up, turns me around, and breaks the mood that is holding me back. Sometimes I have to laugh because I do not know the answer to this question. This question is like a key that opens all doors. Yet no one ever gave me this key. Though I try, I cannot give it away, nor put it down, *nor* pick it up. I think there are no doors to be opened.

When I first came to see you, you gave me the "Dropping Ashes on the Buddha" kong-an, but along came the "Who am I?" kong-an and took its place. Though I sit and think what can I do to instruct this fellow attached to emptiness who drops ashes on the Buddha, always I have to ask, "Who am I?" that instructs and "Who is it?" that drops ashes. When I ask such questions, even the Buddha disappears.

> Dropping ashes
> on sitting Buddha.
> Cleaning ashes
> from sitting Buddha.
> One man drops;
> Another man cleans.
> Ten thousand kalpas
> Before either fool understands.
> Today the sun is shining;
> After my bath
> I dry my hair in the sun.
>
> Love,
>
> Terry

Dear Terry,

Thank you for your beautiful letter. How are you?

Who are you? Give me only one word! Many words are not necessary. Understanding cannot help you.

I know your don't-know mind. One more step is necessary. You said you think you are the question, that it helps you when you are depressed, discouraged, or egotistical and that it is like a key that opens all doors. That is correct. But don't hold your feelings; don't hold your understanding. Put it down. Then when you drink water, you understand by yourself whether it is hot or cold. Then your correct direction clearly appears. Then no problem.

I gave you "Dropping Ashes on the Buddha." That is homework. Don't keep homework in your mind. Only go straight, don't know. When this don't know becomes 100 percent strong, then a good answer to your homework will appear by itself. So it is very important not to hold anything, not to make anything, not to attach to anything—only go straight, don't know. Even Buddha's speech and God's speech—throw it all away. Also throw away your homework. Then you will find the key to the True Empty Gate. If you open the True Empty Gate, then you will get everything. This is most important. That is the first course. Be very careful. Don't attach to the True Empty Gate. So I ask you, "What is the True Empty Gate?" Tell me! Tell me! If you open your mouth, I hit you. If you hit the floor, I hit you. Any action, I hit you. What can you do?

Your poem is not good, not bad. Please make a poem after you finish the "Dropping the Ashes on the Buddha" kong-an. If you make a poem before you finish this kong-an, you will only lose your energy. It is not necessary. OK?

Again I ask you: Someone comes into the Zen Center, smoking a cigarette, blowing smoke, dropping ashes on the Buddha. What can you do? This man is very strong. To any speech or action of yours, he will only hit you. If you don't understand, only go straight, don't know. Don't make your understanding. Your understanding cannot help your true self. If you don't make anything, then this kong-an is no problem. This kong-an is a great love, great compassion, great bodhisattva way kong-an. So only try, try, try for ten thousand years nonstop.

I hope you always keep don't know, which is clear like space, soon finish the great work of life and death, get enlightenment, and save all people from suffering.

Yours in the Dharma,

S.S.

Dear Soen Sa Nim,

While doing work Zen at my desk, the following answer came:

ME: You, stop that.

CIGARETTE MAN: *Hit*

ME: If that is true, the ash and the smoke, are they the same or different?

CIGARETTE MAN: *Hit*

ME: You understand only ash, no smoke.

CIGARETTE MAN: *Hit*

ME: Ashes fall down, smoke goes up, the truth is just like this.

My little daughter is practicing the mantra. Yesterday I asked her why she still sleeps with a stuffed (toy) dog. She said, "I like the dog. It has a very clear mind. It understands it is just a stuffed dog."

I need some strong word medicine. Could you please send me some?

> With hands palm
> to palm,
>
> Bob

Dear Bob,

How are you? Thank you for your letter.

My answer is late, but you said you wanted strong medicine— this lateness is strong medicine. Your answer to the cigarette kong-an is OK, but even if you give him your last answer ("ashes fall down . . .") he will hit you, even harder than before. What can you do? More hard training is necessary.

Your answer is like a mute having a dream. He understands the dream, but he cannot teach other people.

I hope you only go straight, don't know, keep a mind that is clear like space, soon get enlightenment, and save all people from suffering.

Yours in the Dharma,

S.S.

Dear Soen Sa Nim,

Good morning! It is always a good morning somewhere. I am in the morning sun just outside my door, feeling the warmth and the breeze.

New Moon Ocean rolls in and springs onto the rocks. Birds passing through stay a while, singing their own songs. Others build nests to continue birds. Springtime it is and always is somewhere, like the sun is rising while it's setting and setting while it's rising. Like life to death and death to life. Coming and going is all the same.

Dear Soen Sa Nim, your letter is making me very happy. Thank you deeply for giving me so much. I bow to you.

Ever since sitting this morning I have felt like talking with you. It came to me that the man who is putting ashes on the Buddha is no other than ME-Jo-EGO.

You say that I must teach him to make him see his bad actions—to make him realize. So I must teach me to be aware of my own actions—"watch my step."

And this Jo or ME, which is which, is HIT.

Which is the true eye of the thousand eyes? HIT.

This man has been around for eons of time. His name is Karma, my karma. I need to help him do as my Zen master says: "Always keep a mind that is clear like space, soon finish the great work of life and death, get enlightenment, and save all people from suffering." Thank you, Soen Sa Nim.

Yours,

Jo

Dear Jo,

How are you? Thank you for the beautiful letter. You talked about the morning. . . . How are you this morning?

The *Diamond Sutra* said, "All formations are transient. If you view all appearance as nonappearance, you can see your true self." This means, in your mind, don't be attached to anything. Then you can see, you can hear; everything, just like this, is the truth. You say, "Birds . . . build nests to continue birds. Springtime it is and always is somewhere, like the sun rising while it's setting and setting while it's rising." Finally you said, "Like life to death and death to life. Coming and going is all the same." The name for that is nirvana. You already attained nirvana—how happy does this make you?

Your cigarette man answer is wonderful. However, how do you fix his mind? How do you correct him? This is bodhisattva action. You already understand your true way, but this man has a long way to go. You must correctly teach him.

I hope you soon find someone to watch your house so you can come and do a retreat with us.

I hope you always keep a mind that is clear like space, soon finish the great work of life and death, get enlightenment, and save all people from suffering.

Yours in the Dharma,

S.S.

Dear Soen Sa Nim,

Thank you for the teaching.

During the interview yesterday, you gave me the "dropping ashes" problem for homework. Here is my answer: "Keep empty-mirror mind." Since this person is attached to his understanding, trying to teach him by any method will only provoke him to hit. Since he is attached, he will suffer. Sometime he may meet someone keeping clear mind and not suffering and then ask for teaching. Trying to change him might be an attachment to another understanding.

You also said that when I answered this problem, you would give me a "big homework." If this is the answer, or not, I see that "just keeping empty-mirror mind" is good homework.

Yours in the Dharma,

Roger

Dear Roger,

Thank you for your note at the Cambridge Zen Center.

You said your "Dropping Ashes on the Buddha" answer is "empty mirror." You make "empty mirror," so you have a problem. This man is very attached to the primary point. You say, "Empty mirror," so you have already opened your mouth. This is a mistake, so this man hits you thirty times. What can you do? In true empty mirror, there is no speech, no words.

How to understand this kong-an? It's like this: The first time you go to a market with a child, the child doesn't understand anything. He takes some things—chocolate, gum—and puts them into his pocket. You see this and are very angry. "Don't take that!"

The child says, "Why not?"

If you are too strong, the child will cry. You must use soft teaching. First you must pat his head and say, "You are a good boy. First you pay money, then you can have these things. This store's things are not your things. If you take these things, you will become a thief. Do you want to be a thief?"

Then the child says, "Oh, I don't want to be a thief." He understands.

The point is "good boy" and "thief." These two phrases will help in teaching the child. You must check *Dropping Ashes on the Buddha*.* There are one hundred titles. If you keep don't-know mind 100 percent and check the one hundred titles, then one title will appear and help your answer.

You said if you answered your homework, I would give you "big homework." Don't hold homework; don't attach to home-

---

*Soen Sa Nim often tells his students working on this kong-an to check the one hundred titles in the table of contents to his book *Dropping Ashes on the Buddha* (Grove, 1976) for a hint to this kong-an.

work. Only go straight, don't know. Try, try, try, everywhere, all the time. That is most important. If you are attached to homework, you cannot find a good answer. If you only go straight, don't know, then soon a good answer will appear by itself.

I hope you only go straight, don't know, which is clear like space, soon finish the great work of life and death, get enlightenment, and save all people from suffering.

Yours in the Dharma,

S.S.

Dearest Soen Sa Nim,

I cannot answer the kong-an because there is no man dropping ashes on the Buddha. The grass is green, the sky is night, and I love you.

Marge

Dear Marge,

Thank you for your letter. How are you lately?

You say, "I cannot answer the kong-an because there is no man dropping ashes on the Buddha." I say, if somebody comes to the Zen Center, smokes a cigarette, and blows smoke and drops ashes on the Buddha, what can you do? So *if*, OK? If you understand, OK; if you don't understand, only go straight, don't know. Don't check your mind, don't check your feelings, don't check anything. Only go straight.

I ask you, "Why is the grass green? Why is the sky night?" Tell me, tell me, quickly, quickly.

Here is a poem for you:

> The stone girl,
> Walking around everywhere,
> Wants to find her baby.
> Sun shining but no shadow.
> The wooden dog barking,
> Mu, mu, mu,
> The blue mountain
> Puts on a white cloud hat.

I hope you will soon get enlightenment.

Yours in the Dharma,

S.S.

SEVENTH GATE
Ko Bong's Three Gates

The First Gate: The sun shines everywhere.
Why does a cloud obscure the sun?

If you are thinking, you won't understand. If you are attached to words and speech, then you will have a hindrance. Don't attach to the Zen master's speech or anyone's speech. A Zen master often uses bad speech to check his student's mind. Why is this? Is it good or bad? Is it correct or not correct? This is an opposites question. If the wind comes up, maybe a cloud will cover the sun. But this style of thinking is no good. Keep your mind clear, then just perceive, just intuit.

The Second Gate: Everyone has a shadow
following them. How can you not step on
your shadow?

How can you step or not step on your shadow? Why does the cloud cover the sun? These are both opposites questions. The questions are designed to check the student's mind. Usually in day-to-day life, we keep an opposites mind: I like, I don't like; coming and going; good and bad; why and how. Here we are working with opposites thinking. If you completely become one mind, there are no opposites. Then intuition is possible. A kong-an is like a person fishing with a baited hook covered with very tasty food. If the fish is hungry and wants something, it will touch the hook and be caught. Usually our minds want something: I want hard training; I want to become a good Zen student; I want to be correct moment to moment; I want to give a good answer. So you *want*; it may not be a bad want—perhaps it's a good want—still you *want*. Whether it's good or bad doesn't matter, already you are dead. Don't make anything, just do! So I ask you, "How can you not step on your shadow?" If you don't keep a clear mind, you will touch the hook and have a problem.

> *The Third Gate: The whole universe is on
> fire. Through what kind of* samadhi *can
> you escape being burned?*

There are rockets that can deliver hydrogen bombs anywhere on this earth. If someone pushes the wrong button, the bombs will explode and our world will disappear. At that time, everything will be fire; how can you stay alive? When you are doing something, just do it!

Dear Soen Sa Nim,

How are you? By the time you get this, the Orient Express Zen Center should be back in L.A. How wonderful! We send our love and thanks to all of you for your hard work.

I've just finished a twenty-one-day retreat up north, and I'm sending you some poems and some homework. You gave me a schedule, two hours of sleep, practice, two and a half hours of sleep, and one thousand bows—which helped me a lot. Thank you very much. Also, Kwan Seum Bosal helped me, and so did a bunch of mice and the trees. Now I'm happy—wonderful!

Thank you for your most generous and patient teaching. I am grateful to you.

With love and respect,

Sherry

Morning river
Many trees, green, yellow, red
Very clear.
Gloop. Gloop.
River rises on rocks.
Winds come.
Green, yellow, red disappear.
Where are the trees?
Appear? Disappear?
SHHH! SHHH! SHHH!
Half-moon floats near.
Catch it! Catch it!
Sun rises.
Time for morning bows.
    Round yellow mushrooms,
    Red leaves falling
    Geese crying in the cold air—
Is this not enough?
KATZ!
Mouse runs by—
Move your foot.

1. The sun in the sky shines everywhere. Why does a cloud obscure it? Today it is raining.
2. Everyone has a shadow following them. How can you not step on your shadow? Step, step, step.

3. The whole universe is on fire. Through what kind of samadhi can you escape being burned?

[Answer deleted]*

Dear Sherry,

Thank you for your wonderful letter. How are you and Lawlor and the Zen Center family?

Your poems are wonderful. Here is a poem for you:

> Very clear everything
> Green, yellow, red disappear
> Shhh, shhh, shhh!
> Sun rises
> Time for morning bows.
>
> Not enough!
> Not enough!
> Not enough!
> What more do you want?
> The mouse bites your toe!
> OUCH!!

As for your kong-an answers:

1. One more step because no more rain—then what?
2. Also one more step because you are only writing "step, step, step."
3. Wonderful! 100 percent.

------

*The answer was correct, therefore we have deleted it so as not to spoil the fun of generations of Zen students. —Ed.

I hope you only go straight, don't know; which is clear like space, become a number-one Dharma teacher; soon get great love, great compassion, and the great bodhisattva way; and save all people from suffering.

Yours in the Dharma,

S.S.

Dear Soen Sa Nim,

How are you? I hope you are very well and send you my very best wishes.

I have been looking at Ko Bong's "Three Gates" and the other kong-ans too. To me, it looks like this:

1. A cloud obscures the shining sun because that is the nature of a cloud.
2. How can you not step on your shadow? By keeping the direction up to the sun.
3. Through what kind of samadhi can you escape being burned? Maybe "becoming fire" is samadhi? I don't know.

Dear Soen Sa Nim, I know how much you have to do. But if your time allows you to give me a short answer, it would be a big help to me again. Thank you very much.

All my best wishes to you.

In the Dharma,

Ingrid

Dear Ingrid,

Thank you for your letter. How are you? Merry Christmas and Happy New Year.

You sent me answers to "Ko Bong's Three Gates." These gates are very high-class kong-ans. When your consciousness computer becomes high class, then this kong-an is possible. But if your consciousness computer is not so clear, then this kong-an is very difficult.

First: You say, because this is the nature of the cloud. You are attached to the cloud. We say, the dog runs after the bone.

Second: You say, by keeping the direction up to the sun. You have become a statue; how can you save all beings? So I say to you, you are hitting the moon with a stick.

Third: You say, "I don't know." That is a very good answer, but you must cut "I." You don't understand I, so don't use I—only don't know.

These are very difficult kong-ans. There are Ten Gates. You check each gate. Then when you almost finish the Ten Gates, you will understand "Ko Bong's Three Gates." If your Dharma is not strong and you only check the kong-ans, that's just more thinking. Then only your dry cognition thinking will grow, which is not so good.

Again I tell you: don't check your feeling, don't check your mind, don't check your understanding, and don't hold anything. Only go straight, don't know. Try, try, try for ten thousand years nonstop. Then anyplace, any condition, any situation is no problem. OK?

I hope you only go straight, don't know, which is clear like space, soon finish the Ten Gates of Mind Meal, get enlightenment, and save all people from suffering.

Yours in the Dharma,

S.S.

Dear Soen Sa Nim,

Thank you for that wonderful letter. I call it a letter and give it an adjective at the risk of your stick. You say you don't know anything about poetry (and what a laugh as you said so), and of course it's true. Don't know *is* your poetry. And also it's what for convenience I sometimes call mine. A remarkable (sometimes I think the most remarkable) American writer of the last century, Thoreau, said in criticism of the lives that most everyone seemed to feel that they *had* to lead, "How can a man find his ignorance when he has to use his knowledge all the time?" I think he meant, *ignorance* is something close to your (and my) and his don't know. Thank you for pointing to that don't know—how wonderful that it begins everywhere and has no beginning!

I keep saying thank you and, of course, can't say (nobody can) what I'm thanking you for. Speaking, as you do, from your own clear mind, your words seem to refer with special aptitude to the most specific circumstances of my own life. At the moment, we're deep in a very old and complicated karma of mine, a place where I've spent a great part of the past twenty-three years but had not seen for three years. A good place to look at karma and recognize don't know, don't know.

And your kong-ans. But I'll save those for the end. I have to tell you what a great pleasure it was to have that photograph of the visit, with you and Linc and Aitken Roshi and Maezumi Roshi—I think we are in danger of being spoiled. But it's a great pleasure to think of you being able to work together, of that contact between the different branches of the Zen Dharma being possible, instead of the sectarianism that sometimes mars and limits even the great traditions.

The readings you mention: I try to keep them to a small number every year (and not even every year) and do them at about the same time. They're part of my way of earning a living and, at the same time, a way of meeting younger people. You know about that. But I find it hard to talk about poetry, and my own in particular; I think it would be a mistake for me to try to *talk* about it too much, any more than I would want to talk about Zen in public. And the travels—what shall I say? They're karma for the present, and I see that. What I don't know about them neither comes nor goes. As for where my head is, the answer is where the question is.

What an exciting suggestion of yours, that maybe someday we would teach the Dharma together here. It would be a great place for it in many physical respects, and I wish we could entice you over for a visit—maybe you and Aitken Roshi together, though he says he can't make it this year. Please tell Mu Gak Su Nim that I'd love to hear from him. How was his retreat? I think of it often. The house we're in is an ancient stone farmhouse surrounded by sheep pasture. I realize that in the absolute, one place is as good for practice as another, but in some respects, relatively, this is better than some, as situations go: quiet, the ancient walls, the closeness of the season. I try not to waste too many thoughts imagining it as a small *zendo,* but there's a chronic temptation to do that. Trying not to be attached to the idea nor even to the nonattachment.

Those kong-ans—and thank you, with a deep bow, for them. "Ko Bong's Three Gates":

The first one ("The sun in the sky shines everywhere. Why does a cloud obscure it?") First answer: I hit the floor. Second answer: I think so.

Second kong-an ("Everyone has a shadow following them. How can you not step on your shadow?") First answer: I hit the floor. Second answer: Walking through the empty sky. Where is the empty sky? I hit the floor.

Third kong-an: ("The whole universe is on fire. Through what kind of samadhi can you escape being burned?") First answer: I hit the floor. Second answer: Burning.

And then Nam Cheon to JoJu ("If you completely attain the true way of not thinking, it is clear and empty as space. So why do you make right and wrong? What did JoJu attain?") First answer: I hit the floor. Second answer: Nothing whatever. Nothing special.

Thank you, then, once more. May your teachings wake us all to ourselves or teach us to wake ourselves.

Thank you,

William

Dear William,

How are you and Dana? Thank you for your wonderful letter. I thought you were very busy, but you sent me a long letter. You make me so happy. Now I know your news and your experiences and your practicing.

In each sentence, your mind appears. That is your opinion. But this opinion is shining to others' minds, so they understand what is the true direction. So you are already a great bodhisattva. You said don't know is wonderful, that it has no beginning and no end. This is correct. Also, don't know has no ignorance and no knowledge, also no Buddha, no God, no mind, and no universe. But don't be attached to don't know. ONLY DON'T KNOW IS DON'T KNOW, which is just like this.

Just like this is: ignorance is ignorance; knowledge is knowledge; Buddha is Buddha; God is God; mind is mind; universe is universe. One by one, each thing is complete. Which means don't know is complete. Then you are complete. Then everything is complete. Therefore, a dog barking, a chicken crowing, and a car horn honking are all the truth. Already you understand. So we say don't know means put it all down. Don't check your mind and feelings—only go straight.

You said it was wonderful that teachers from different branches

67

of the Zen tradition can work together. That is the correct opinion. That is wonderful. Your mind and my mind are the same. When I was in Los Angeles, Aitken Roshi and Maezumi Roshi came to Tahl Mah Sah Zen Center and we had a very good time. At that time, I found that it was possible to work together with Maezumi Roshi and Aitken Roshi. Also, our direction is the same direction—very wide, not narrow.

Some Zen masters do not send their students to other Zen centers or allow them to have interviews with other Zen masters. If they have interviews with another Zen master, they will cut them off as their student. Their style is very strong, very narrow. They don't understand wide space and infinite time. Their karma becomes hard and heavy. Finally, they cannot move. They are like wine that has gone sour. Nobody will drink it.

But we are already doing together action. Maezumi Roshi's students, Aitken Roshi's students, and my students all can visit each others' Zen centers with no problem or hindrance. So I met you, and now I am sending you a letter. How wonderful it is!

You said that too much talking about poetry is not helpful, but if you don't give talks, young people will not understand poetry. This is Zen. Zen and poetry are the same. We say, if you open your mouth, I will hit you thirty times; if you close your mouth, I will hit you thirty times. This is like using makeup. If you use too much, the face doesn't look good. If you don't use enough, the facial features are not clear. But if you use the correct amount of makeup, then the eyes, nose, and lips are all clear, and everyone will like this face and follow it. This is like your speech. Our Zen practicing and teaching are the same way.

I hope that someday you, Aitken Roshi, and I will be able to teach together.

You described where you are staying. This is also wonderful. I would like to visit your place someday. The place where you practice is very important. But most important is this: moment to moment, how do you keep just-now mind? This means, moment to moment, you must keep your correct situation. Then anyplace, anytime, you have no problem.

Your kong-an answers are not good, not bad. However, understanding cannot help you. You must attain these kong-ans, which means that these kong-ans are just-like-this kong-ans. In just-like-this kong-ans, hitting the floor is not necessary. Hitting the floor is primary point. If you attain primary point, that is called first enlightenment. Next is "like this." Here is an example: The sky is blue; the tree is green; three times three equals nine. This is like this. If you attain like this, this is called original enlightenment. If the question is a wide question, then primary-point and like-this answers are OK. But if the questions are one-pointed (for example, "Is this a bell or not?"), then hitting the floor or saying, "The sky is blue, the tree is green" is not correct. Only ring the bell. One action. This is correct. This is just like this. If you attain just like this, this is final enlightenment.

Ko Bong's three gates are one-pointed questions. So you must only give one word or one action, which is a just-like-this answer. For just-like-this answers, only one answer is necessary—not two. I will give you a hint.

First gate: When you turn on the light, what? When you turn off the light, what?

Next, the second gate: Don't check anything; only go straight. This means don't make anything, then you will get the correct answer.

Third gate: I hit you. Then what do you say? If you touch fire, what do you say? The whole universe is on fire. What can you do?

These hints mean there is no subject, no object, no inside, no outside—only become one. So becoming one means that only a one-word or one-action answer is necessary. This is the correct situation at that time.

Next, Nam Cheon–to–JoJu answer. Hitting the floor is wonderful. But next, "Nothing whatever, nothing special" is a big mistake. These are thinking words. In Zen, there are two kinds of words: dead words and live words. Dead words are opposites-thinking words. Live words are hit opposites, hit–inside-and-outside, become-one words. For example, someone asked Dong Sahn Zen Master, "What is Buddha?"

He said, "Three pounds of flax." At that time, he was weighing flax—just three pounds—so inside and outside were only three pounds of flax. Also at that time, his correct situation was three pounds of flax.

I ask you: What are you doing now? Don't make dead words. Just now, what is your correct situation? *This* is JoJu's attainment, also your attainment, also all eminent teachers' attainment. This is truth; this is the great way.

You say sometimes, "I don't know," and you say, "I know." That is OK. Only go straight, don't know. Then you will understand don't know. That means don't know is don't know. You are don't know; don't know is you. So don't know means you understand you. You understand you means, you are you. In other words, don't know is don't know, so I say: Only go straight, don't know. Then everything you see, everything you hear is the truth. The blue mountain does not move. The white clouds float back and forth. Only "just like this."

I hope you always go straight, don't know, keep a mind that is clear like space, soon finish the great work of life and death, get enlightenment, and save all people from suffering.

Yours in the Dharma,

S.S.

Duk Sahn Carrying His Bowls

One day Duk Sahn came into the Dharma room carrying his bowls. Sol Bong, the housemaster, said, "Old Master, the bell has not yet been rung, and the drum has not been struck. Where are you going carrying your bowls?"

Duk Sahn returned to the master's room. Seol Bong told Am Du, the head monk, what had happened. Am Du said, "Great Master Duk Sahn does not understand the last word."

When Duk Sahn heard of this, he became very angry and sent for his head monk, Am Du. "Do you not approve of me?" he demanded.

Then Am Du whispered in the master's ear. Duk Sahn was relieved.

The next day on the rostrum, making his Dharma speech, Duk Sahn was different from before. Am Du went to the front of the Dharma room, laughed loudly, clapped his hands, and said, "Great joy! The old master has understood the last word! From now on, no one can check him."

There are three questions from this story. First: The Zen master did not understand the last word. What was the last word?

Second: What did Am Du whisper in the master's ear?

Third: How was the master's speech different from before?

This is a very famous kong-an in China, Korea, and Japan. In the first question, the last word means correct situation, relationship, and function. In other words, Am Du was saying that his teacher didn't understand his correct situation, relationship, or function.

What did Am Du whisper? The words were of two kinds. At first Duk Sahn Zen Master was very angry. You must take away his angry mind. It is like a wife and a husband: they love each other very much, but one day the wife says to her husband's friend, "My husband did such and such." Then her husband hears that and is very angry at his wife. "Don't you believe in me?" If you were the wife, what could you do? What would you say to your husband? First, you must give him good speech. Second, you must make the correct situation clear; just saying you're sorry is not enough.

If you were Am Du, the head monk, then you would first have to make your correct relationship with the Zen master clear. Then the Zen master would understand, and his angry mind would disappear. Second, you would have to offer correct teaching about the last word, then the Zen master would be completely relieved.

How was Duk Sahn's speech different than before? Before, Duk Sahn didn't understand the last word; now he understands the last word. Before, what kind of Dharma speech did he give? His Dharma speech before doesn't matter. At this time, what kind of Dharma speech did he give? This is a very important point. If you finish all three questions then you can understand correct situation, relationship, and function. That means you understand the last word. Then you can become a great Zen master.

Why did so many problems appear in this kong-an? Duk Sahn Zen Master returned to his room without saying anything. He was asked where he was going carrying his bowls, but he only returned to his room. That was a mistake. The drum had not yet been struck, and yet he carried his bowls to the Dharma room. This was not correct. At that time, if you were the Zen master, what could you do? One clear sentence to the housemaster is necessary. Whether it is a mistake or no mistake doesn't matter. If you make a mistake, use your mistake and make it correct. Then the house-master could say, "Oh, Zen Master, now I understand! Thank you very much." Then the housemaster would not have spoken to the head monk and the problem would not have appeared.

So one final question is: If you were the Zen master and some-one asked you where you were going carrying your bowls, what could you do? This question is a little difficult, but you must attain this!

Dear Master Seung Sahn,

Thank you very much indeed for your strong and helpful letter. I meant to reply to it some time ago, but it came just before I left for India, and although I took it with me, I had very little opportunity to answer it and, in fact, thought it best not to, because the Indian scene needed to be accepted very simply on its own level with full attention. And that remark will at once show you that I did not go instantly to the answer of the bowls—if I had, your letter would have been easily replied to in India—so whatever answer I give you will, I expect, be inappropriate.

But this doesn't matter. I would like to explain, if I may, what living with the Indians and traveling with them in trains and buses helped me to see. First, that there are few barriers of understand-ing, even of language, when one is really sincere. And second, that this applies even more when one gives oneself to the occasion completely, even if very simply. This was brought home to me forcibly on one occasion. Quite early on in my stay, I was walking through a crowded street with an English couple. Biddy, the wife, was in a wheelchair, as she suffers from arthritis, and her husband was pushing her. There was a little gap in the crowds; an Indian came past us, and as he looked down at Biddy, an expression of great compassion came into his face—instantly, with no thought—and he said some sort of blessing and walked on. What struck me was the instantaneous, pure compassion, perhaps because it is what I lack. My tendency is to analyze and discriminate before I give, and that was a great lesson to me in just pure giving.

It changed things for me in India. I have a tendency—out of self-regard—to want to write a good speech before I give it and thus to make sure that I shall not let myself down. But after that incident, I found much greater freedom to talk without notes, to just be myself and thus forget myself, to be easily close to people and at one with what I was doing. In a way, that's why I didn't reply to your letter. Things were working of their own accord, and I didn't want the formalization of a kong-an; it seemed inappropriate. Because what pleased me more than anything was the easy simplicity of it. There were not particular states or experiences; it certainly had nothing to do with satori, but it was a practical working loose from self-imposed restrictions, and I needed that very much.

If anything, it made me feel that *all* religious ways and methods were inappropriate and make no hoot of difference, and that what really matters is something far, far simpler, which has nothing to do with any method, but just has to do with being who you are without any fear. Then there is no point of passing kong-ans or in gaining recognition of any sort. For what can it matter if I am wrong or right about a kong-an, so long as I am able to be open and entirely sincere with whatever person I talk to? For the last twelve years, I have loved Zen and lived on Zen in the form of the old masters' writings and my own experience of turnabout in my mind. But now it is as though the word *Zen* could be dropped from my vocabulary without any trouble.

I would like now to return to your letter and thank you again for your kindness in writing such a good and detailed letter. I would like to think that just being simple approximates to your number-four state, because it seems to be what you describe—just doing what one does and being what one is, only really engaged on it, not from any idea.

I can't answer the kong-an. Master Duk Sahn sounds as though he was carrying his bowls rather purposefully, as though he were rather overinvolved with carrying bowls and thus overinvolved with ideas of the world and himself, but I don't know what the last word could be. If I were Am Du, I think I would whisper, "Drop the bowls without any clatter," meaning, "Let go your hold on ideas of yourself but without causing any trouble to the world as you do so—no fuss." Then the master's speech would be fearless and sincere, which could certainly be different from speeches drawn from ideas, even if those ideas were good ones.

The time is growing short now until you arrive, and we look forward to it very much. If you have time to reply to this letter before you go, I would be delighted and very pleased, but if you do not have time, it does not matter a scrap.

Yours in the Dharma,

Anne

P.S. As I had specifically asked you for a kong-an, I sound more than ungrateful in this letter for not paying it very much attention. Please overlook this rudeness, which is tantamount to dropping the bowls with a clatter, and please understand that it was unintentional.

Dear Anne,

Thank you for your letter. How are you and your husband?

In your letter, you said you visited India and returned. When you were in India, you had many, many good experiences. You talked about the Indian man who offered a blessing for Biddy. That is Indian mind. In India, there are many rich and high-class people and poor, low-class people; it is very wide. They all understand enough mind, which is "What is life?"—a philosophical mind—and "What is truth?" So they don't care about their position. High-class, rich, low-class, poor—it doesn't matter. They understand what is most important. That is giving mind. Giving mind is great-love mind, great compassion, and the great bodhisattva way. You already experienced that. That is wonderful.

In my last letter, I told you that a kong-an is not special. Moment to moment, keep correct situation, which means when you are doing something, you must just do it. Then seventeen hundred kong-ans are no problem. Also, a good answer, a bad answer, or even no answer doesn't matter. How much do you believe in yourself? That is very important. If you believe in yourself 100 percent, then you can see, you can hear, you can smell, and you can taste clearly. Then when you are doing any action, just like this is truth. That is a true, live kong-an. You already said, "Then there is no point in passing kong-ans or in gaining recognition of any sort. For what can it matter if I am right or wrong about a kong-an, so long as I am able to be open and entirely sincere with whatever person I talk to?" So I say to you, you are wonderful.

Sometimes, though, we have a bad backseat driver. This backseat driver controls our original master. There are three kinds of this: the first six consciousnesses, which control the body and its senses; the seventh consciousness, discriminating consciousness—

like and dislike; and the eighth consciousness, the storehouse or memory consciousness. These backseat drivers want to control your master. If your master is strong, then the backseat drivers cannot control your car. But if your master is not strong, these backseat drivers will always control your car and you will have many problems. You must control these backseat drivers. Then these backseat drivers will listen to your master and help you. Then any condition, any situation is no problem. Then when you see, hear, smell, touch, even think, everything is the truth. Nam Cheon Zen Master said, "The true way is not dependent on understanding or not understanding. Understanding is illusion. Not understanding is blankness. If you attain truth, it is clear like space." There is no subject, no object, no inside, no outside. Inside and outside become one. If somebody is hungry, feed them. If somebody is sick, only pray to help them. It is like that Indian man. That is great love, great compassion, and the great bodhisattva way.

You already said, "I would like to think that just being simple approximates to your (just-like-this) state, because it seems to be what you describe—just doing what one does and being what one is, only really engaged on it, not from any idea." This is called simple mind. Very old people, about two hundred years ago, understood Taoism, Confucianism, and Buddhism very well. They controlled their understanding, so their minds were very simple, which means their understanding and their actions became one. Nowadays, people understand too much. They don't practice, so they cannot control their understanding. They become very complicated. This means their understanding's direction is one way and their action's direction is another way. So they check . . . check inside and outside. They are holding something, making something, and attached to something. They are very busy and can't control their minds. Because of this, they are afraid, confused, angry, full of desires, ignorant, sad . . . a lot of suffering. In the end, some people even kill themselves! That is the modern world's sickness. Nobody guarantees our life. When you die, where will you go? What is life? What is death? These are very basic questions. If you finish these important questions, you are completely free and you will get true happiness. You will get everything!

Modern people like freedom and want happiness. But they don't understand what complete freedom and true happiness are. They only understand freedom and happiness based on some outside circumstance related to relationships, politics, wealth, or health. Those kinds of freedom and happiness are based on something that will change, an outside situation. This kind of freedom is not freedom; there are many hindrances. Outside happiness is not true happiness; there is still a lot of suffering. That comes from where? It comes from holding their idea, holding their situation and condition. If their opinion, condition, and situation disappear, then correct opinion, correct condition, and correct situation will appear. Then if they die after one hour, no problem. If you keep "enough mind" moment to moment, this is possible. In Taoism it is written, "If I hear the true way in the morning and if I die in the evening, it is no problem." But originally our true self has no life, no death— that is Zen. If you attain your true self, you will get freedom from life and death and true happiness.

The Duk Sahn kong-an: Your answer is not good, not bad. Don't be attached to the kong-an. If you keep your mind like a clear mirror, then a good answer to the kong-an will appear by itself. The first question is: What is the last word? Am Du's saying, "Great Zen Master doesn't understand the last word" means that Duk Sahn Zen Master doesn't understand the correct situation, which means he doesn't understand that "just like this" is truth. When you reread the kong-an, then you can soon find Duk Sahn's mistake. Duk Sahn's action, if he hadn't made a mistake, is the last word, which means, moment to moment, keeping a correct situation. The name for that is just like this. Next, Am Du whispered in the master's ear. First, the Zen master was very angry: "Do you not approve of me?" So you must first make this angry mind disappear. Next, you must teach him the correct situation. The last part is "How was Duk Sahn's Dharma speech different from before?" What is Duk Sahn's understanding? Then you will understand how Duk Sahn's Dharma speech was different from before. All of this is very simple. If you think, or if you check, you make complications and don't understand. Cut off all thinking and only perceive the kong-an. It is like keeping your mind clear when you are doing something, just do it. That's all.

Kong-ans are not special. Also, they are not necessary. Not only kong-ans, but all Zen masters, all buddhas, and all eminent teachers are not necessary. Only go straight, keep a don't-know mind. This don't-know mind understands everything and fixes all of the mind's sicknesses. So how strong and complete is your don't-know mind? That is very important! Don't know is not don't know. Don't know is primary point. Don't know is everything. But don't know is don't know. So only go straight for ten thousand years nonstop. Try, try, try, then you will get everything.

I hope you always go straight, don't know, which is clear like space, soon finish the great work of life and death, get enlightenment, and save all people from suffering.

Yours in the Dharma,

S.S.

————————————

Dear Soen Sa Nim,

How are you? Thank you for your guidance and encouragement during our three-day meditation retreat. I am still the frustrated frog—if I could leap out of the well, I would believe in myself 100 percent. I have a high fever, but I am drinking *hot* tea and covering myself with a heavy blanket. I understand this *medicine* is necessary!

Here is an answer to the kong-an on which I am working, "Duk Sahn Carrying His Bowls."

What is the last word of Zen?

[Answer deleted]

What did Am Du whisper to the master?

"Master, I hope you are feeling well this morning."

As you advise, I am just going straight ahead . . . only what am I? (A frog with a fever.) See you soon.

Respectfully,

Steve

Dear Steve,

How are you now? Thanks for your letter.

You say you are still the frustrated frog, you want to leap out of the well, and then you would believe in yourself 100 percent. I say to you, don't make anything; then you will get everything. If you want something, then you already have made a mistake. What is believing in yourself 100 percent? What are you?

You already understand. Nothing at all. Just like this. Just-like-this mind is clear mind. Clear mind means, moment to moment, you must keep your correct situation. Then everything is OK. What more do you want? Put it all down. A good answer or a bad answer to kong-ans doesn't matter. Only keep just-now mind. If your mind is not moving, there is no problem. Good answers and bad answers are not important. Most important is how do you keep just-now mind?

Regarding your kong-an answers: Your "last word" answer is wonderful. But in "What did Am Du whisper in the master's ear?"

you don't understand the correct situation at that time. Zen Master Duk Sahn shouted to Am Du, "Do you not approve of me?" He was *very* angry! Also, the Zen master doesn't understand the last word. If you understand this situation correctly, then you will understand the correct answer.

I hope you always keep your correct situation moment to moment, soon finish the great work of life and death, and save all people from suffering.

Yours in the Dharma,

S.S.

Dear Soen Sa Nim,

How are you? How is your body? We are all saying Kwan Seum Bosal for you to get a healthy body again and help us to save all people. Rane, our new baby, says, "Waaaaa!" She is wonderful and we are enjoying her very much, but she is very demanding.

I will see you Saturday and then at the Yong Maeng Jong Jin (meditation retreat) in Providence.

Kong-ans I'm working on . . .

#8. What is the last word?

[Answer deleted]

What did Am Du whisper in the master's ear?

[Answer deleted]

How was the master's speech different?

Yesterday was Monday. Today is Tuesday.

Yours in the Dharma,

Bob

Dear Bob,

How are you and Marilyn and Rane? Thank you for your letter. My body is no problem—very strong, because you tried much special Kwan Seum Bosal for me. Thanks again.

Congratulations on the birth of your baby. That's wonderful. How is Marilyn's health? I hope she is always strong, so Rane will also be strong. In Korea, when a baby is first born, it cries, "GUAAA!" *Guaaa* means "Save me! Help me!" This is Gua. In Korean, *a* means "I"; *gu* means "save" or "help." In other words, "This world is an ocean of suffering, and I just came into it, so please save me from this ocean of suffering." That is the first sound of all babies. Is it correct? You must save your baby. That is the correct way; this is great love and the great bodhisattva way.

Great interview means moment-to-moment interview. This means your don't-know mind is having a moment-to-moment interview with you. So no interview means great interview. If always and everywhere don't know and you become one, then you will get happiness always and everywhere. Then any action, any thinking, any idea, any condition, any situation is no problem. That is enough mind. If you have enough mind, any action, any idea can help other people. So this is the great bodhisattva way and great love.

Regarding your kong-ans: First, your last-word answer is wonderful. Next, your whispered answer. You're almost done, but your answer is like somebody with a good head, good clothes, good shoes, but no necktie. Finally, how was the master's speech different? You're scratching your right foot when your left foot itches. This means you only understand like this; you don't understand just like this.

I hope you always are keeping a mind that is clear like space, soon finish the great work of life and death, become a great man, and save all people from suffering.

> Yours in the Dharma,
>
> S.S.

Dear Soen Sa Nim,

This is the second day of our retreat in Cumberland.

About that carrying the bowls kong-an:

If my teacher asked, "Do you not approve of me?" I would hit him. "Why make 'you,' 'me,' 'approve'? Just like this—when the meal bell is rung, carry your bowls."

Hello to you and the Empty Gate people.

> With much love
> and respect,
>
> Carole

Dear Carole,

Thank you for your letter. How are you? You said you were at a YMJJ at the Providence Zen Center. That is wonderful.

Your answer to the carrying the bowls kong-an is not good, not bad, but not clear, which means it's not a bull's-eye. The Zen master's job is to use anything to make correct. If you make a mistake, use that mistake to make correct. If you have good or bad, use good or bad to make correct.

Before, I told you about my teacher, Ko Bong Sunim. Anytime there was a bad situation for Man Gong, his teacher and my grand teacher, Ko Bong would say, "Man Gong doesn't understand the Dharma. Man Gong's teaching is bullshit." One day Man Gong heard that and went to Ko Bong's room. "Why do you have bad speech for me?" he shouted. Then Ko Bong saw his mistake and used that mistake to make correct. "Zen master," he said, "I do not have bad speech for you . . . only for Man Gong." Then Man Gong smiled, very happy. "You are tired now," he said. "Sleep, sleep," and he went away. Thus, Ko Bong used his mistake to make correct.

If Duk Sahn Zen Master says to you, "Do you not approve of me?" what can you do? Tell me! Tell me! If you don't understand, only go straight, don't know. Then your consciousness will work completely and correctly. Then you will get the correct answer.

I hope you only go straight, don't know, which is clear like space, soon finish the great work of life and death, and save all people from suffering.

Yours in the Dharma,

S.S.

NINTH GATE
Nam Cheon Kills a Cat

*One day Nam Cheon Zen Master was in
his room when he heard a big commotion
outside. The 250 monks of the western hall
and the 250 monks of the eastern hall were
fighting over a cat. Nam Cheon became
very angry, picked up this cat, and said,
"You! Give me one word, and I will save
this cat! If you cannot, I will kill it!"*

Here Nam Cheon is checking the students' minds to see if they
truly love the cat or if they are only attached to the cat. If they are
only attached to the cat, they cannot answer. If they are not attached to the cat—if they love the cat—then saving the cat's life is
possible. But none of the monks said anything. There was only silence. So finally Nam Cheon Zen Master killed the cat.

*In the evening, JoJu, Nam Choen's top stu-
dent, returned to the temple. Nam Cheon
told JoJu everything that had happened.
When he was done speaking, JoJu took off
his shoes, put them on top of his head, and
walked away. Nam Cheon Zen Master
then said, "If only you had been there, I
could have saved the cat."*

The first question: When Nam Cheon Zen Master holds up the cat and says, "Give me one word, and I will save the cat. If you cannot, I will kill it!"—what can you do? This is a love kong-an. If you have great love and great compassion, then this kong-an is no problem.

Here is a hint: A long time ago, during the time of King Solomon, there was an argument between two women about a baby. Each claimed it was her baby. So King Solomon said, "Bring this baby, and I will divide it in two. Each of you can take half." Then one woman said to the other, "Oh, you take the baby. It is yours."

Then who was the true mother? To King Solomon, it was very clear. This is a love story. If you have great love inside, then you have a Zen mind.

Unconditional love means great love, great compassion, and the great bodhisattva way. So unconditionally sit; unconditionally DO IT! Unconditionally practice. Don't check your condition. This is great love. If your mind is unconditional, then this unconditional mind has no I, my, or me. I do everything for all beings—for husband, for wife—that is great love. If you have this mind, it is possible to save the cat.

The second question: JoJu walked away with his shoes on his head. Then Nam Cheon Zen Master said, "If you had been here, I could have saved the cat." What does this mean? Why did JoJu put his shoes on his head and walk away? What does this mean? If you attain this kong-an, then you attain great love, great compassion, and the great bodhisattva way. This means moment to moment, keep your correct situation, correct relationship, and correct function.

Dear Soen Sa Nim,

How are you? Today I will take the Precepts at Providence. I am writing you, though, because soon you will travel to Korea, and I will return to school. So for a long time, I won't see you. I had planned to sit during the Labor Day retreat at PZC [Providence Zen Center], but that weekend my father is getting married, so I must be with him.

Maybe you will check my homework anyway, "Nam Cheon Kills a Cat." To master Nam Cheon, I would say, "It's theirs!"

Thank you very much for giving the New Haven Zen Center so much of your time this summer. Since you came those two weeks in a row, we've had many new people come to practice, including many of my classmates. Perhaps when school starts again the Zen Center will be very busy.

See you in December.

Yours truly,

Erik

Dear Erik,

Thank you for your letter. How are you? Congratulations on taking the Five Precepts.

You wanted to come to the retreat but you cannot—that's OK. What is most important, moment to moment, is keeping your correct situation and relationship. Your father is getting married, so you will stay with him. That is the correct situation and correct relationship. That is Zen, not special.

To Nam Cheon's kong-an you say, "It's theirs." If only you and someone else (two people) are present, that answer is possible. But at the time there were 500 people together, 250 from the eastern hall and 250 from the western hall. The other students don't like your speech; they say, "NO!!!" Then what? You cannot act.

One more step is necessary, then you will correctly understand great love and great compassion and attain them. This answer is not your idea—you are a thief because you took this answer from the story of King Solomon.

Again I ask you: Zen Master Nam Cheon, holding up the cat, says, "You! Give me one word, and I will save this cat. If you cannot, I will kill it!" What can you do? Tell me, tell me! If you don't understand, only go straight, don't know. OK?

I think that in the future the New Haven Zen Center will become stronger and a wonderful Zen Center, because you are strong, very clear, and have many friends.

I hope you only go straight, don't know, which is clear like space, soon finish Nam Cheon's kong-an, get enlightenment, and save all people from suffering.

Yours in the Dharma,

S.S.

Busy Beloved Soen Sa Nim,

Not knowing where you are, hopefully this reaches you before your world trip. Thank you for your helping answer letter.

Now Nam Cheon's cat was saved from the beginning, but to save the cat and all cats, my one word is *meow*.

—MEOW
Yours truly,
Patricia

Dear Patricia,

Thank you for your letter. How are you and your family?

Your answer is not good, not bad. We say 90 percent. There is 10 percent missing because our kong-an has two kinds of answers: "subject just like this" and "object just like this." For example, when you are hungry, then what? You must eat. This is subject just like this. When someone else is hungry, then what? This is object just like this. That is called the correct situation. When you are hungry, what is your correct situation? When someone else is hungry, then what is your correct situation?

So Nam Cheon's kong-an is not subject just like this. If it were, your answer would be 100 percent. But it is an object just-like-this kong-an, so your answer is not enough. Somebody is hungry, and you say, "I am hungry too." You are not keeping your correct situation. You must have great love, great compassion, and the great bodhisattva way. Then this kong-an is no problem.

If you don't understand, you must see a cowboy movie. You can find two kinds of cowboy stories: money and love. Money stories are not interesting. You must check a love story. Then you will see that this love is without conditions. That is true love. If you find that, then this kong-an is no problem.

Only understanding cannot help you. You must be without conditions and find true love, that's great love, great compassion, and the great bodhisattva way. That is also everyday mind and Zen mind.

I hope you only go straight, keep a clear mind, attain Nam Cheon's kong-an, and save all people from suffering.

Yours in the Dharma,

S.S.

Dear Soen Sa Nim,

Thank you for the delicious ginseng tea. It tastes especially lovely in this weather.

I was glad to find you in stronger health than the last time I treated you, and good to know you have been in the expert hands of advanced Korean acupuncturists. For myself, I have studied only ten years and know I am still a beginner—as with Zen—nothing can be rushed too much, but if I continue, I shall get more and more intuition "by natural process."

You mentioned that you "have" diabetes. But I ask, "Are diabetes and you the same or different? Is not diabetes only a symptom of karma that one develops and by the same token can eliminate—nothing special?"

It is said we get energy from food, air, and exercise, and depending on each person's karma, perhaps they need to eat different food, do different exercises, etc., to eliminate old patterns and get balance within themselves.

It seems our bodies are our friends, and they will tell us what is correct or poisonous for us. It is hard sometimes to listen.

When old karma is so ingrained, we do not see it and get confused by our own delusions; then we need a teacher to point out the way. I am very grateful to you for your help and look forward to the retreat you suggested when I get back from China.

For a few weeks now, I will take a break from usual work, as even what one cares for can get stale if pursued too consistently.

So you asked how could I save Nam Cheon's cat?

HA HA HA
Lovingly, yours in the
Dharma,

Carole

[This letter is typed on a piece of paper on which Carole has drawn a big circle with diluted red ink.]

Dear Carole,

Thank you for your letter and circle. How are you?

You like ginseng tea; that's wonderful. Also, you said you were just a beginner in acupuncture. If you always keep a beginner's mind, then already you are complete. In Korea they say if you try something for two years, you will attain something. That means you have already studied acupuncture for ten years, but you are still keeping a beginner's mind. A beginner's mind is a complete mind—wonderful.

You ask whether diabetes and I are the same or different. I hit you. This morning I took fifty units of insulin. Do you understand? Diabetes has helped me very much and has also helped other people very much. It also helps you.

You talked about getting energy from food, exercise, etc. and said that people need to do different things, depending on their karma, to find a balance. Also, you said our bodies are our friends and they will tell us what is correct or poisonous. All of that is correct.

Our body is our house. If you take care of your house, your house will stay strong and beautiful, no problem. If you do not take care of your house, it will soon become dirty, have problems, and will not be so beautiful. If you are attached to your body, however, you become your home's attendant. If you become only an attendant, that's a hindrance and a problem.

Zen mind means finding the correct function for any karma, any condition, any situation, and making the correct relationship and situation. Then, as you already said, a balance is possible. It is also possible for you to change any condition and situation. So

Zen mind means not checking anything, only keeping the correct situation moment to moment.

Sometimes you like special things. Special is not bad, not good, but if you are attached to special, then this special will kill you. Why did you make this circle? What does it mean? Is this a number or not? Which one? Tell me, tell me! If you say it is a number, I'll hit you; if you say it's not a number, I will also hit you. What can you do?

Your answer to Nam Cheon's kong-an is "HA HA HA." You must check your consciousness. When you make "HA HA HA," the cat is already dead. This cat kong-an is a great love, great compassion kong-an. That means you must keep the correct situation and correct relationship. If somebody is hungry, do you say, "HA HA HA"? Is that correct? You give them food. That's the correct relationship and correct situation.

So if somebody is about to kill a cat, only "HA HA HA" is not enough. You must understand great love and great compassion, then a correct answer will appear. So again I ask you: Nam Cheon holds up a cat and says, "Give me a word, and I will save this cat. If you cannot, I will kill it!" What can you do? If you don't understand, only go straight, don't know. Try, try, try for ten thousand years nonstop. Don't check your understanding, OK?

I hope you only go straight, don't know, which is clear like space, soon finish the great work of life and death, attain the cat kong-an, get enlightenment, and save all people from suffering.

Yours in the Dharma,

S.S.

Dear Soen Sa Nim,

Thank you for writing Jeffrey and me.

This card is in honor of your kong-an "To Kill a Cat"! I see why "meow" is not a good answer, and I agree "so what—that doesn't mean anything when a cat is about to die or be saved." It reminds me of the Biblical story of King Solomon solving a dispute between two women who both claim possession of a baby. "It's mine!" said one. "No, mine!" said the other. "OK," Solomon said, "we'll cut it in half and give you each a half." "Well, all right," said one. "No, no, let her have it!" said the other, at which point Solomon knew who the real mother was. But I surely don't have enough compassion to understand either of your kong-ans, beyond the fact that hot and cold kill the little me. I relate everything to my small self but do not have enough confidence to come from an inner center that's large and open, that embraces the world. Little by little, though. It's good Jeff and I are married; we help give each other perspective when we each get off the track!

I would like to meet you sometime. Jeff and I planned to attend the three-day sesshin in Berkeley for our honeymoon, but the volcano and earthquakes kept us from traveling. Much to do here instead. Yes, I think sometime soon we will be inviting you to Seattle for a visit!

> Very best wishes
> and "metta,"
> Francie

Dear Francie,

Thank you for your letter and beautiful cat picture. How are you and Jeff? You talk about the cat kong-an and the story of King Solomon solving a dispute between two women who both claimed possession of a baby. Yes, they are similar. But the story of the two women is very simple; there were only two people involved, so only one person's idea is possible. But in the Nam Cheon kong-an, many people were fighting, and so one person's idea is not possible. Only if you have great love and great compassion is it possible to save this cat. Again I ask you: Nam Cheon is holding up this cat: "You! Give me one word, and I will save this cat! If you cannot, I will kill it!" What can you do? How much love do you have?

We say, without idea, without condition, without situation—the name for this is great love and great compassion. You must keep this mind. Only go straight, don't know. This is not difficult. Don't know has everything. Don't know makes everything. Don't know is complete. Don't know is absolute. So only go straight, don't know. Then you will get everything, OK?

I hope you only go straight, don't know, which is clear like space, soon find your correct direction and truth and correct life, help your marriage, get enlightenment, and save all people from suffering.

Yours in the Dharma,

S.S.

Dear Soen Sa Nim,

Rain falls on the dark streets below.

Thank you for teaching me about true medicine at the New York retreat.

You said, "Form is emptiness; emptiness is form.

No form; no emptiness.

Form is form; emptiness is emptiness.

Which is correct?"

I said, "All are no good. Wall is white; mat is yellow."

You said, "Correct! Only keep this mind. This is true medicine."

Now I take this medicine many times each day and am beginning to feel very healthy. This health means *attunement:* mind, body, universe work together and become one.

Today, some fellow medical students asked me to be president of the Medical Committee for Human Rights (MCHR). I want to help them learn about true medicine.

Yesterday, I got a really good haircut by a barber master from Greece.

For the cat-cutting kong-an I say,

Put it all down!

Still raining,

Matthew

Dear Matthew,

Thank you for your beautiful true medicine letter. How are you?

You are wonderful. Now you are a complete doctor. A complete doctor means both outside and inside, so you are a complete doctor. You are going to medical school. This is the outside-doctor course. Also, you already have attained "All are no good. Wall is white; mat is yellow." This is the inside-doctor course. So outside and inside are now no problem, which means that saving all people is possible. That is great love, great compassion, and the great bodhisattva way. Only go straight. . . . What are you doing now? OK?

About the cat kong-an: What is the correct situation at that time? You are attached to "Put it all down." These are very dangerous words. Somebody is very sick and you are the doctor. Is "put it all down" OK? At that time, what is the correct doctor's situation? *Doctor* means great love job, great compassion job, and great bodhisattva job. If you put this all down, someone will die. OK? I say, not OK.

You must give me a good answer. If you don't understand, only go straight, don't know. Don't lose this medicine, OK? Don't use "put it all down." Put-it-all-down medicine is medicine for people who think too much. You already have correct direction. One more

95

step, then you will find the correct answer. Tell me! Tell me! Hurry up! Hurry up!

I hope you always have correct medicine, soon get enlightenment, and save all people from suffering.

Yours in the Dharma,

S.S.

Dear Soen Sa Nim,

"Nam Cheon Kills a Cat."

"You! Give me one word, and I will save this cat! If you cannot, I will kill it!"

Later, JoJu took off his shoe, put it on his head, and walked away. Nam Cheon said, "If you had been there, I could have saved the cat."

If JoJu had been there, he would have understood the situation clearly: that all sentient beings need to die first in order to be saved. So he would have yelled, "KILL!" and thus saved the cat's life, because Nam Cheon would not need to really kill it; one person understood what was necessary.

When JoJu passed by, after Nam Cheon did kill the cat, he took his shoe and put it on his head, as he would at all funerals.

A cause-effect thought has been with me for some time now. How incredibly artless our world would be with no suffering. Look at all the beauty that has come from pain music, song, dances. . . . There's a part of me that exalts these forms, which would probably die out if we all were enlightened. I'd be totally bored of listening to serene music all the day!

Have a nice trip on the East Coast.

Alicia

Dear Alicia,

How are you, Alicia? Thank you for your beautiful letter.

First, Nam Cheon's kong-an.

You say, "KILL." You understand more than JoJu and Nam Cheon. Very good. But before you open your mouth, Nam Cheon has already cut out your tongue, and it has fallen to the ground. Your understanding cannot help you. How can you save this cat? Tell me! Tell me! Only one word!

Your next answer is not good, not bad. You say, funeral. What is the meaning of a funeral? You only explained. In Zen, explanations are not necessary. Explanations are all dead words. Live words are necessary. You must find live words. What is a funeral?

You say art comes from suffering and beauty comes from pain. That is correct. Pain, suffering . . . then art and beauty appear. But what is true art? What is perfect beauty? Where does suffering come from? Who made pain?

If you understand these original points, then you are complete. Your art will help many other people and give them great joy, and your beauty will give many people great happiness. Your suffering will give other people great love, and your pain will give other people great compassion. You will get the great bodhisattva way. The bodhisattva way tastes like water; you say, boring.

I hope you already have boredom. If you keep boring mind anyplace, anytime, then everything will be no problem. So only go straight, don't know, soon get true boredom, finish the great work of life and death, and save all people from suffering.

Yours in the Dharma,

S.S.

TENTH GATE
Mouse Eats Cat Food

The mouse eats cat food, but the cat bowl is broken. What does this mean?

What does this mean? You may understand, but understanding cannot help you. You must *attain,* and then this kong-an will become yours. This kong-an is a subject just-like-this kong-an. Mouse, cat food, bowl, broken—four things. For example, your stomach is not feeling very good and you want ice cream. Then, "Oh, I have some money. I can get some ice cream." You go to an ice cream store and buy ice cream. You eat it and feel very good! Wonderful! So money buys ice cream; ice cream into your stomach, then a wonderful feeling! So the money is changing, changing—wonderful. Mouse, cat food, cat bowl, broken . . . then what?

Most people are too clever. Very clever means they don't understand. You must become stupid; then you can get the point of this kong-an. This kong-an is very easy—too simple. Can you see your nose? "Yes, I can see my nose." Can you see your eyes? Not possible! If you want to see your eyes, you must put down your want-to-see mind. Then you can attain your eyes. It is the same as if you want to understand your mind—it is not possible. You must *attain* your mind. Someone may say, "I have already attained my mind." That is not possible; that is crazy! That is a clever mind. To become stupid means to have a simple mind. Thinking mind becomes don't-know mind, becomes simple. Stupid people only DO IT! The clever mind is always checking, checking, checking or holding something or attached to something. If you want to understand this kong-an, you must become completely stupid, a complete rock head.

Dear Soen Sa Nim,

Thanks for your good answer.

The koan: "The mouse eats cat food, but the cat bowl is broken." My answer was "Mice are gray, the sun comes up in the east, my socks are red, the cat bowl lies on the floor." You said, "This is scratching your left foot when your right one itches." My new answer is "The mouse is full, the cat is hungry."

I will always consider you *my* Zen master, as I learned more in our few meetings than in seven or eight years under several masters. *Thank you!*

Is there some special way to understand 0, 90, 180, 270, 360 koans and the typical responses to each? I could not (due to workload) be at the morning discussion. I'm like the cigarette guy in the *zendo*—I understand empty; I know the sun comes up in the east; when I'm thirsty, I drink. But I'm attached to desire—particularly sex and freedom. Since I consider *you* my real master, I shall follow your advice.

> The sun is setting
> The clouds are beautiful

> Hapchang,

> Jack

Dear Jack,

Thank you for your letter.

You say, "The mouse is full, the cat is hungry." I say, "The dog runs after the bone." You must find the meaning behind the words of the kong-an. There are four things: mouse, cat food, cat bowl, broken. You must ask what this mouse is, what this cat food is, etc. Check these four things and find the meaning behind them. As for your answer—how did you understand that the mouse is full and the cat is hungry? *You* make the mouse full; *you* make the cat hungry. So I hit you thirty times.

You said thank you for what you learned in our few meetings. You're welcome. You must do some hard training, then you will understand me. If you don't understand Zen, you can't understand me. You must be a good Zen student.

You wrote:

> The sun is setting
> The clouds are beautiful

I wanted to write these very words, but you took the words out of my mouth. So I have nothing left to say. But I ask you not to lose the mind that wrote these words.

See you soon,

S.S.

Dear Soen Sa Nim,

I have just finished *Dropping Ashes on the Buddha,* which I read with great interest.

My answer to "The mouse eats cat food, but the cat bowl is broken": Cat food is mouse food, so the mouse bowl is intact.

Sincerely,

Joyce

Dear Joyce,

How are you? Thank you for your letter. You say you read *Dropping Ashes on the Buddha*—that is wonderful.

You sent an answer to the mouse kong-an. If you're thinking, you won't understand this kong-an. It's a very high-class kong-an, like calculus in mathematics—very difficult. This means that first you must go to elementary school, then middle school, then high school, and finally college. The cat-food kong-an is like college work.

First you must understand primary point, then like this, then just like this. If you don't understand just like this, you cannot understand the mouse kong-an. Here is the primary-point course:

$$3 \times 3 = 9$$
$$3 \times 3 = 10$$

Which one is correct? If you pass this, then I will ask you the next course, OK?

I hope you will send a good answer to me. If you don't understand, only go straight, don't know. Don't check anything. If you're thinking, you won't understand. Thinking answers cannot help you.

Yours in the Dharma,

S.S.

Dear Soen Sa Nim,

How are you? Five years ago, you asked me, "The mouse eats cat food, but the cat's bowl is broken. What does it mean?" Today I answer—AWAKE!

Here are two poems for you.

The Buddha said, "I am not God, not Buddha,
I am only awake."
I hit Buddha thirty times.
Before the stone dog had its jaws locked around a bone.
Now the keen-eyed lion is looking at who threw the bone.

* * *

The sky is clear and blue in New Haven.
I hit myself thirty times.
JoJu's laughing donkey has a *powerful* kick.
Smog alerts in Los Angeles—
No problem, I've come home.

This don't-know baby finally took its first step. Thirty deep bows in your direction. See you soon.

Bob

Dear Bob,

Thank you for your letter. How are you and your family?

You often come to Tahl Mah Sah Zen Center. You make me so happy.

Your homework answer was "AWAKE!" Not bad, not good. But

your answer is like scratching your right foot when your left foot itches. This kong-an is a subject just-like-this kong-an. For example, a quarter is twenty-five cents, twenty-five cents buys ice cream, ice cream goes into the stomach, and the mouth says, "Wonderful." So the quarter changes to wonderful. You must understand that. If you don't understand, only go straight, don't know, try, try, try for ten thousand years nonstop. OK?

Your poem is wonderful. Here is a poem for you:

> The Buddha said, "I am not God, I am not Buddha."
> The sky is blue, New Haven is west.
> The stone dog bites the keen-eyed lion.
> Smog in Los Angeles, Tahl Mah Sah no problem.

I hope you only go straight, don't know, which is clear like space, soon finish the mouse kong-an, become a great man, and save all people from suffering.

Yours in the Dharma,

S.S.

Dear Soen Sa Nim,

How are you? Thank you for your letter. My family is good, but my wife is very tired from too much work and too much small children's needs. A vacation is soon necessary in the mountains. Then I will stay for a few weeks for retreat.

My homework—

The mouse eats cat food, but the cat's bowl is broken.

Delicious!

Here are two more poems for you:

Quarter = twenty-five cents = ice cream = stomach = wonderful!
Ah!
A stone cat growls in the shadows,
But the mouse has enough mind—
How delicious the cat food tastes.

* * *

Ten thousand years is a very long time
Each instant is ten thousand years.
Crack! Boom!
A streak of lightning pierces the frozen sky.
See Hoy, Sumana, Bob only go straight
moment . . . moment . . . moment.

I hope to see you in September before you go to Korea. I will be back in L.A. around September 10.

Yours in the Dharma,

Bob

Dear Bob,

Thank you for your letter. How are you and your family?

Regarding the mouse kong-an: not good, not bad. But your answer is still like scratching your left foot when your right foot itches. One more step is necessary. Only go straight, don't know.

Your poem is wonderful. Here is a poem for you:

Quarter = twenty-five cents = ice cream
Into stomach—have much energy.
Everything is clear.
Wind blowing.
All flowers bowing, bowing, bowing.

I hope you always go straight, don't know, soon finish the mouse kong-an, get enlightenment, and save all people from suffering.

Yours in the Dharma,

S.S.

Dear Soen Sa Nim,

How are you? Thank you for your reply to my letter.

I am like a man in a dark room looking for his lost money. After a long search, the coins are tightly within his grasp, but it is still a little difficult to sort the dimes from the pennies. So again, my homework—

The mouse eats cat's food but the cat's bowl is broken.

Quarter = twenty-five cents = ice cream = stomach = Wonderful!

Mouse = cat food = cat bowl = broken = Free!

Here is a poem for you:

> When one sees smoke over the mountain, it
>   means fire.
> When one sees the mouse, how can all four
>   matters become clear?
> CUT!
> The golden wind blows through the barren trees,
> Appearing in the east, disappearing in the west—
> The mouse cuts the strings and is free from all
>   restrictions.

Thank you for your picture. See you soon.

Bob

Dear Bob,

Thank you for your letter. How are you and your family?

In your letter, you said you are like a man in a dark room looking for his lost money. After a long search, he finds the coins but it is still difficult to separate the dimes and pennies. Nirvana and enlightenment are the same as that. Nirvana is when you cannot separate any name and form, which means direction is not clear. Enlightenment is when each thing appears completely clearly. So maybe you only got nirvana, not yet enlightenment. One more step is necessary. The sun rises over the eastern mountains in morning; dimes and pennies are clear.

Regarding your answer to the mouse kong-an: it is not good, not bad. Your answer is like hitting the moon with a stick.

I hope you only go straight, don't know, which is clear like space, soon finish the great work of life and death, get enlightenment, and save all people from suffering.

Yours in the Dharma,

S.S.

Dear Soen Sa Nim,

Your koans are ringing in my head, waves of sound. I don't know? Who doesn't know? Know? No! Circumstances are such that I cannot come to see you in the East. KATZ! But I will work hard on my koans and take paper *sanzen*.

As for your mouse and the cat's broken bowl. When the mouth wants to speak about it, words fail; when the mind seeks affinity with it, thought vanishes.

Knew what I think. I don't know!

I hope that all is well with you and your disciples. Here is a poem for you:

> Blue ink touches white paper
> A faucet drips drip, drip.

If you were here, I would gladly let you rain blows on my head; since you are not here, I rain blows on yours. KATZ!

Steve

Dear Steve,

I will hit you thirty times!! Put it all down!! Originally there is no coming or going or staying or arriving. This is infinite time and infinite space. You already have freedom, so if you come, it's good, and if you don't come, it's good. Only this.

Your KATZ! How many pounds does it weigh? If you open your mouth, I will hit you thirty more times.

If you like letter interviews, I like them too.

About the mouse who eats cat food: There is a meaning behind the words. If you are attached to the words, you don't know this meaning. What is mouse? What is cat bowl? What is broken? When these four things become one, then you will have true meaning.

I hope you do more hard training, finish your homework soon, attain enlightenment, and become a great man.

Your poem is very good, but Buddha doesn't understand it— and neither do I. Here is a poem for you:

> Original face is clear
> on the green pine and white rocks.

If you want to understand what this means
you must understand that a quarter is twenty-five cents.

You have a freedom arm—sometimes short, sometimes long.
My arm is not a freedom arm. I want to hit you, but I can't reach
that far. So I will say that I am sorry.

> See you later,
>
> S.S.

To Ven. Seung Sahn,

You said in your last letter that there is a great place to fall down
(pitfall) in the sentence I wrote you: "The sky after rain is blue, and
the falling sunshine is warm." "Please find the falling place," you
said. I venture to give my answer that the falling down is the earth.
   I await your kind instruction as ever.

> Thank you,
>
> Satam

At a corner, in the garden of the International Buddhist Meditation Center.

To Rev. Satam,

Homage to the Three Treasures.
   I give you thirty blows.

Where is the pitfall (the falling place) in the statement? The cat is taking a nap in the sunshine, and the hen is scratching the ground.

Where is the falling place? Don't be attached to the words.

What happened to your previous homework? If you solve the homework—that is find out how to cure the man who drops ashes on the Buddha's image and understand the kong-an of the cat's bowl that is broken—then you will be able to solve a million kong-ans and a million falling places. I wish you would soon solve them and be able to deliver deluded sentient beings.

Here is a hint about the kong-an of the cat's bowl being broken: $3 \times 3 = 9$. $5 + 4 = 9$. $10 = 1 + 9$. $18/2 = 9$.

Though the statements are different, the answer is the same: 9. Therefore the answer is 9. The mouse, the cat's food, the cat's bowl, broken: these four words are different, but it is the same place they return to.

So long,

S.S.

Dear Soen Sa Nim,

Hello! Thank you for the wonderful precepts and Dharma teacher ceremonies a few weeks ago. It makes me deeply happy to be with you and with all our family together—and it was so much fun!

Here's some homework for the mouse-eats-cat-food kong-an:

> THIS CORPSE IS VERY HUNGRY,
> SO FIRST SHE EATS HER THUMB,
> SHE NIBBLES ON HER FINGERS,
> AND SWALLOWS DOWN HER BUM.

SHE GOBBLES ALL THE BUDDHAS,
AND BODHIDHARMA TOO,
AND YOU'D BETTER WATCH OUT,
SOEN SA NIM, CAUSE NOW
SHE'S EATING YOU!
CRUNCH. CRUNCH. CRUNCH.

Yours in the Dharma,

Sherry

Dear Sherry,

How are you and Lawlor and your family? Thank you for your letter.

Your homework about the mouse kong-an was not good, not bad. One more step is necessary. Somebody asks you if this is a bell or not. At this time, do you say, "I eat you!"? Is that correct or not? Only ringing the bell is correct. For a one-point question, a one-point answer is necessary. A quarter is twenty-five cents. Twenty-five cents buys ice cream. Ice cream is all in the stomach, good feeling, wonderful! The quarter changes around and around and becomes wonderful. The mouse changes around and around, then what? You must find this!

Where is your cigarette man kong-an? First you must finish the cigarette man kong-an; then the mouse kong-an is very easy. But originally all kong-ans are your moment-to-moment correct situation. The mouse kong-an is about the correct mouse situation at that time. In the cigarette kong-an, this man does not understand the correct situation. You must teach him the correct situation, which is the correct relationship to Buddha and the ashes. He doesn't understand, so you must teach him very softly. This man has a lot of pride, so first you make "good boy, good boy" speech; then maybe he will listen to you. OK?

If you don't understand, only go straight for ten thousand years nonstop! Try, try, try!

I hope you always keep don't-know mind, become clear like space, soon finish the great work of life and death, get enlightenment, and save all people from suffering.

Yours in the Dharma,

S.S.

ELEVENTH GATE
Man Gong's Net

One day, Zen Master Man Gong sat on the high rostrum and gave the speech to mark the end of the three-month winter retreat. "All winter long you monks have practiced very hard. That's wonderful! As for me, I had nothing to do, so I made a net. This net is made out of a very special cord. It is very strong and can catch all buddhas, patriarchs, and every human being. It catches everything. How do you get out of this net?" Some students shouted, "KATZ!" Others hit the floor or raised a fist. One said, "The sky is blue, the grass is green." Another said, "Already got out. How are you, great Zen Master?" From the back of the room, a monk shouted, "Don't make a net!" Many answers were given, but to each, Man Gong only replied, "Ah ha! I've caught a BIG fish!" So how do you get out of Man Gong's net?

This is a very famous kong-an. Zen Master Man Gong always taught his students not to make anything. If you practice strongly, don't make anything, and don't want anything, then you can attain no hindrance. Then this kong-an is not a problem. But if you are thinking, if you still have I, my, me checking mind, then you cannot get out of the net. This net is life and death and includes everything. Even if you are Buddha, if you have thinking, you cannot escape the net.

Man Gong's net is an attack kong-an. "I caught a big fish" is a strong teaching style. It drops down a large (000 size) hook for you. If you touch this fishing hook, you will have a big problem! It's just like a boxing match: hit, hit, hit . . . then you must defend yourself. So how do you hit Man Gong's net? How do you take away Man Gong's idea? Man Gong's idea made the net, so you must hit that.

Kong-an practice is very important—it means put it all down. In Zen we say, if Buddha appears, kill the Buddha; if an eminent teacher appears, kill the teacher; if demons appear, kill them. Kill everything that appears in front of you. That means don't make anything. If you make something, then you have a hindrance. If you can completely put it all down, then you have no hindrance and your direction becomes clear. So our practicing direction is to make our situation, relationship, and function in this world clear. Why do you eat every day? If that is clear, then your life is clear and you can help this world. Moment to moment, our job is to do bodhisattva action and help all beings. Man Gong's net makes our direction and its function clear. Only help all beings. But that is just an explanation. Explanations cannot help you! An answer is necessary.

Seung Sahn's Three Men Walking

Three men are walking. The first man
makes a sword sound; the second man
waves his hands; and the third man picks
up a handkerchief.

1. If you were there, what would be your correct function?
2. What is the relationship?
3. And lastly, what is the situation?

If you pass all Ten Gates, then this world will become yours. Becoming yours means you will attain the function of freedom from life and death. Then correct function, correct relationship, and correct situation are possible. If you pass these Ten Gates, then I have a present for you, the Twelfth Gate.

A long time ago, Cheung Sahn Zen Master would frequently ask his students this kong-an. Nobody understood. Sometimes he would use wild actions or shout, "Yahhhh! Why don't you understand?" Still they couldn't answer completely.

This kong-an is very important. It's an object just-like-this-style kong-an. There are two kinds of just-like-this kong-ans, subject and object. Subject just like this means when you are hungry, what? Eat! Object just like this means if someone is hungry, what? Give them food! That is object just-like-this style. So in this kong-an, what is your correct function? These three men do different actions, but the situation is the same. Their function is different, but it is the same situation. What is their relationship? What is the situation? Same situation, same condition, same relationship, but the function is different: one makes a sword sound, one takes out a handkerchief, one waves his hands—different action, but the meaning is the same.

Here's a hint: You go to a theater where somebody is doing a one-man show. He tells a very funny story, he acts funny, talks funny, and then everybody laughs. Everybody is happy. Many different people are laughing with different styles. Somebody is laughing, "Ha, ha, ha, ha!" Somebody else is laughing, "Hu, hu, hu, hu!" Somebody else is laughing, "Ho, ho, ho, ho!" Different laughing styles. The action is different, but the condition and the situation are the same. So what kind of condition, what kind of situation, what kind of relationship? You must attain that. That is the object just like this.

If you don't understand, just don't understand. If you keep this "don't understand," then your don't-know mind becomes very strong, and a big don't know is possible, which means great question and great doubt. If you don't know completely, then you will get complete enlightenment. If you have only a small question, only small enlightenment is possible. There are many kinds of enlightenment—small enlightenment, middle enlightenment, big enlightenment, and then finally, no enlightenment. No enlightenment is complete enlightenment.

The Third Interview
A Personal Account
—Jerry Shepherd

My heart is pounding in the palms of my hands as I come into the interview room, make my bows, and take my place before Zen Master Seung Sahn.

Entering the third and final interview of the retreat with this man, I am again stricken with awe and, this time, something more: fear. Fear of failing a test I have read about but never faced . . . till now.

I settle my legs, calm my hands, take a deep breath, and wait.

"What is your name?" the master says.

I hit the floor as I have learned to do in the earlier two interviews: an action to cut off thought at the moment it arises.

"Only that?" he asks.

"Jerry Shepherd."

"How old are you?"

I hit the floor.

"Only that?"

"Thirty-eight."

He nods. Clad in his robes, seated on his red mat and cushion, he is a powerful, imposing man—centered, solid, resolute. He has been sitting here, cross-legged, for nearly two hours.

Before him on the floor lies a varnished gnarled wooden stick, a foot and a half long. To the right, in front of the stick, sits his bell. His hands are poised, one on each knee.

He now picks up the stick and holds it before him.

"Un Mun said the Buddha is dried shit on a stick," he says. Then points at the stick.

"Is this a dried-shit stick?"

I answer with a gesture.

"No." He taps my knee with his stick in reprimand: a symbolic thirty blows. "No, no smell," he says. "Is it a dried-shit stick? Is it a dried-shit stick?"

I hit the floor.

"Only that?"

I hesitate, then answer.

"Only that?"

Another answer.

"Yes," he nods. "The sky is blue. What color is the sky?"

Answer.

"Yes. The walls, what color are they?"

He laughs and taps my knee again with his stick: second reprimand. "No."

Another answer.

"Good." He nods, then leans forward on his stick. "Now, a man comes into the temple, smoking a cigarette. He begins to drop ashes on the statue of Buddha. He says if you try to stop him, he will hit you. What do you do?"

My heart thumps once, hard. Then I suddenly know what clear mind is: I have no answer at all.

"This man is dropping ashes on the Buddha. What do you do?"

I answer.

"No." He shakes his head. "No, he will hit you if you do that. You start a fight? Do you understand what I mean by hit?" And he puts his stick over his right shoulder as if preparing to swing at a pitch. "Hit. Hit."

"What do you do?" he asks me again, resting his stick point down on the mat in front of him.

I give another answer, starting to feel disheartened now.

"No," he says softly, shaking his head, then taps my knee again with the stick, another thirty blows. "No. You must have a clear mind. When your mind is clear, it is like a mirror. When red comes, what do you see?"

I answer.

He nods. "When white comes, what do you see?"

Answer.

Nod, eyes closed. "Must have clear mind."

His hands form a *hapchang;* he makes his dismissal bow, rings his bell: the interview is over.

I bow and leave the room, very discouraged.

Halfway back to the Dharma room, I suddenly understand.

APPENDIX 1

Notes on the
Zen Masters of the Ten Gates

JoJu (778-897) Called Chao-Chou in Chinese, after the town in northern China where he lived and taught fot the last forty years of his life. He is one of the most famous Zen masters in the history of the tradition and one of the "superstars" during the golden age of Zen in the Tang dynasty (618–907). He appears in the First and Second Gates.

Seong Am The dates of his birth and death are not known. He was a disciple of Yen T'ou (827–887), who in turn was a disciple of Duk Sahn (Ch., Te-Shan; 780–865) mentioned in the Eighth Gate. Seong Am appears in the Third Gate.

Hok Am (1108-1179) He was a granddisciple of Hsueh Tou, the compiler of the *Blue Cliff Record* (Ch., *Pi-yen-lu;* Jp., *Hekigan-Roku*). He appears in the Fourth Gate.

Hyang Eom (d. 898) Called Hsiang-yen in Chinese, he was a disciple of Kuei-Shan (771–853), who was the founder of the short-lived Kuei-Yang school of Zen and one of the great masters of the Tang era. Hyang Eom appears in the Fifth Gate.

Ko Bong (1238-1295) He was one of the most famous Zen teachers during the Sung dynasty in China (960–1279). Along with Ta-Hui (1089–1163), he provided the creative burst of Zen activity in the last years of the Sung era. He appears in the Seventh Gate and should not be confused with Korean Zen Master Ko Bong.

Duk Sahn (781-867)   Called Te-Shan Hsuan-Chien in Chinese, Duk Sahn was one of the most important Zen masters of the T'ang period in China. He was the teacher of Sol Bong (Ch. Hsueh-Feng) and Am Du (Yen-T'ou Ch'uan-Huo).

Nam Cheon (748-835)   Called Nan-Ch'üan P'u-Yüan in Chinese, Nam Cheon was one of the most famous Zen masters of the Tang dynasty. His most famous student was JoJu.

Korean Zen Master Ko Bong (1890-1961)   The teacher of Zen Master Seung Sahn and a disciple of the famous Zen Master Man Gong (1872–1946), he was famous throughout Korea for his eccentric and unorthodox behavior.

APPENDIX 2
Zen Master Seung Sahn
(1927–2004)

Zen Master Seung Sahn was the first Korean Zen master to live and teach in the West, coming to the United States in 1972. He was born in North Korea near Pyongyong to Protestant parents. He grew up during a time when Korea was under Japanese military rule, when political and cultural freedoms were heavily suppressed. After the Second World War, he studied Western philosophy at Dong Guk University in Seoul but became deeply dissatisfied with his ability to help his country through political activities or academic knowledge. While staying in the mountains at Ma Gok Sah temple, a monk living there introduced him to the Diamond Sutra and advised him to do a long solo retreat if he really wanted to answer the great question of human suffering. Shortly after becoming a monk in October 1948 he began a rigorous hundred-day solo retreat resulting in his enlightenment.

After his enlightenment Zen Master Seung Sahn continued to practice hard to deepen his attainment. He eventually received inka from Zen Masters Keum Bong and Keum Oh and Dharma transmission from his teacher Zen Master Ko Bong in 1949. At twenty-two years of age, Zen Master Seung Sahn had become the youngest Zen master in Korea. After this, he remained in Korea and worked on reforming Korean Buddhism, which had suffered greatly under Japanese rule.

Following his teacher's charge to teach internationally, Zen Master Seung Sahn moved first to Japan and then to the United

States in 1972. As he became more acquainted with the needs of Westerners, he devised methods of teaching that were built partly on his own background in Korean Buddhism and Zen and partly on what was appropriate in the current situation. His interest was always in making Zen Buddhism understandable and relevant in terms of everyday life. Because he was never attached to tradition, he gave Westerners the gift of relevant teaching and forms. He spent the last thirty-two years of his life teaching and establishing over a hundred Zen centers around the world.

Zen Master Seung Sahn is the author of seven books in English: *Dropping Ashes on the Buddha, Only Don't Know, Ten Gates, Bone of Space, The Whole World Is a Single Flower: 365 Kong-ans for Everyday Life, The Compass of Zen,* and *Wanting Enlightenment Is a Big Mistake.* A more complete account of Zen Master Seung Sahn's early life and enlightenment can be found in the last chapter of *Dropping Ashes on the Buddha.*

APPENDIX 3
Glossary

Blue Cliff Record (Ch., *Pi-yen-lu*; Jp., *Hekigan-Roku*) One of the most important collections of kong-ans, compiled in 1125 and still in use today.

Bodhidharma (Skt.) The first Zen patriarch, who reputedly came from China in A.D. 520 and sat for nine years facing a wall at Shao-lin temple.

Bodhisattva (Skt.; lit., *bodhi* meaning "perfect wisdom of prajna," and *sattva* meaning "a being whose actions promote unity or harmony.") One who vows to postpone the still bliss of enlightenment in order to help all sentient beings realize their own liberation; one who seeks enlightenment not only for himself but for others. The bodhisattva ideal is at the heart of Mahayana and Zen Buddhism.

Buddha-nature That which all sentient beings share and manifest through their particular form. According to the Zen school of Buddhism, the Buddha said that all things have buddha-nature and therefore have the innate potential to become Buddha.

Dharma (Skt.) Basically, Buddhist teaching; in a wider sense, any teaching or truth.

Dharma room In Zen Master Seung Sahn's Zen centers, the meditation and ceremony hall.

Dharma teacher   An older student who takes an additional Five Precepts and accepts the responsibility to teach new students about Zen practice.

Five Precepts   The first five lay vows of Buddhism:

> I vow to abstain from taking life.
>
> I vow to abstain from taking things not given.
>
> I vow to abstain from misconduct done in lust.
>
> I vow to abstain from lying.
>
> I vow to abstain from intoxicants taken to induce heedlessness.

Gassho (Jp.)   *See* Hapchang.

Hapchang (Kor.; Jp., *gassho*)   The gesture of placing the hands palm to palm before the chest to indicate respect, gratitude, and humility.

Interview   A formal, private meeting between a Zen teacher and a student in which kong-ans are used to test and stimulate the student's practice; may also occasion informal questions and instruction.

Ji Do Poep Sa   A student who has been authorized by Zen Master Seung Sahn to teach kong-an practice and run meditation retreats because of the strength of his or her practice.

Kalpa (Skt.)   An eon; the time period during which the physical universe is formed and destroyed; an unimaginably long period of time.

Karma (Skt.; lit., "cause and effect")   The continuing process of action and reaction, accounting for the transformation of all phenomena. Thus our present thoughts, actions, and situations are the results of what we have done in the past, and our future thoughts, actions, and situations will be the products of what we are doing now. All individual karma results from this process.

KATZ   The famous Zen belly shout. Its proper use is to cut off discriminative thinking.

Kido (Kor.; lit., "energy way")   A chanting retreat.

Kwan Seum Bosal (Kor.; Skt., Avalokitesvara; Ch., Kwan [Shih] Yin; Jp., Kannon, Kanzeon; lit., "one who perceives the cries of the world" and responds with compassionate aid)   The bodhisattva of compassion.

Mantra (Skt.)   Sounds or words used in spiritual practice to cut through discriminating thought so that the mind can become clear. In some practices, mantra is used to induce various kinds of insight.

Metta   Unconditional and unattached loving-kindness.

Mu Mun Kwan   A collection of forty-eight kong-ans usually studied before the *Blue Cliff Record*. Usually translated as "The Gateless Gate," it was composed in 1229 by the Chinese monk Wu Men Hui-K'ai (1184–1260).

Nirvana   Complete extinction of individual existence; cessation of rebirth; entry into bliss.

Roshi (Jp.; lit., "venerable (spiritual) teacher")   A Zen master.

Samadhi (Skt.)   A state of intense concentration.

Sanzen (Jp.)   *See* Interview.

Satori (Jp.)   The experience of awakening, or enlightenment.

Sesshin (Jp.)   *See* Yong Maeng Jong Jin.

Skandhas (Skt.)   The five aggregates that make up human existence: form, feelings, perceptions, impulses, and consciousness.

Soen Sa Nim (Kor.; lit., "honored Zen teacher")   A Zen master.

Transmission   Formal handing over of the lineage succession from teacher to student.

Yong Maeng Jong Jin (Kor.; lit., "valorous or intrepid concentration," sometimes poetically rendered as "to leap like a tiger while sitting")   In the West, a three- or seven-day silent retreat involving thirteen hours of formal meditation practice a day. Participants follow a schedule of bowing, sitting, chanting, eating, and working, with an emphasis on sitting meditation. Once or twice during the retreat each participant has an interview with the Zen master or a Ji Do Poep Sa.

Zen Center(s)   Residential meditation communities under Zen Master Seung Sahn's direction. Each has daily morning and evening practice open to the public, and every month or two a Yong Maeng Jong Jin is offered in each location.